PYROTECHNIA

OR,

A DISCOVRSE OF

ARTIFICIALL

FIRE-WORKS:

The Naval & Military Press Ltd
© 2008

Published and © by the
The Naval & Military Press
in association with the Royal Armouries

Unit 10 Ridgewood Industrial Park,
Uckfield, East Sussex, TN22 5QE
Tel: +44 (0) 1825 749494
Fax: +44 (0) 1825 765701

MILITARY HISTORY AT YOUR FINGERTIPS
www.naval-military-press.com
ONLINE GENEALOGY RESEARCH
www.military-genealogy.com
ONLINE MILITARY CARTOGRAPHY
www.militarymaproom.com

ROYAL
ARMOURIES

The Library & Archives Department at the
Royal Armouries Museum, Leeds, specialises
in the history and development of armour
and weapons from earliest times to the
present day. Material relating to the
development of artillery and modern
fortifications is held at the Royal
Armouries Museum, Fort Nelson.

For further information contact:
Royal Armouries Museum, Library, Armouries Drive, Leeds, West Yorkshire LS10 1LT
Royal Armouries, Library, Fort Nelson, Down End Road, Fareham PO17 6AN

Or visit the Museum's website at
www.armouries.org.uk

PYROTECHNIA

OR,

A DISCOVRSE OF

ARTIFICIALL

FIRE-WORKS:

In which the true Grounds of that Art are plainly
and perspicuously laid downe :

Together with sundry such Motions, both *Straight* and
Circular, performed by the helpe of Fire, as are not
to be found in any other Discourse of this kind,
Extant in any Language.

VVhereunto is annexed a short T R E A T I S E of *Geo-*
netrie, contayning certaine Definitions *and* Problemes,
for the Mensuration of *Superficies* and *Sollids* , with *Tables* for
the Square Root to 25000, and the Cubick Root to 10000
Latus , *wherein all Roots under those Numbers are*
extracted onely by Ocular Inspection.

VVritten by *John Babington* Gunner, and Student
in the M A T H E M A T I C K S.

LONDON,
Printed by T H O M A S H A R P E R, for R A L P H M A B,
M D C X X X V..

TO
THE RIGHT HONOV-
RABLE, THE EARLE OF
Newport, Maſter of his Majeſties Ordnance,
my ſingular good Lord.

Right Honourable :

Am not induced to preſent this Treatiſe to your Lordſhip for any worth that is either in it, or in my ſelfe, the Author of it; the thing being of ſmall moment, and my ſelfe of as little account : but your Lordſhips ſingular clemency to all, and your Honourable favour vouchſafed to me in particular, hath made me thus bold, and hath cauſed me thus farre to preſume. I have beene for certaine yeeres paſt, and ſo at preſent am, one of the inferiour Gunners of his Majeſtie; and ever ſince I held that place, I have endeavoured to gaine ſuch skill and experience, as I eſteemed moſt requiſite for that ſervice. And to that end I have beſtowed ſome time and expence, as my occaſions and ability would permit, in the practiſe of *Artillery* and *Fire-workes*, wherein though I have chiefly aymed at ſuch concluſions as might be uſefull againſt an enemy in the *field*, yet theſe *halcyon* dayes of peace and tranquility, which

through

through the goodneſſe of God we have ſo long en-joyed, have given mee occaſion to invent and pra-ctiſe ſuch alſo as theſe following: which howſoever they may ſeeme to ſerve onely for delight and exer-ciſe, yet as by the handling of theſe there may bee gained knowledge in the natures and operations of the ſeverall ingredients and their compoſitions; ſo the due conſideration of the ordering of them may excite and ſtirre up in an ingenious minde, ſundry inventions more ſerviceable in times of warre. Now becauſe your Lordſhip hath of late, by the gratious providence of the Almighty, for your ex-traordinary wiſedome and worth, beene advanced to that eminent place, upon which I have ſome de-pendance, and to which I ſtand obliged by my ſpe-ciall ſervice (to which alſo all workes of *Pyrotech-nie* may ſeeme to have relation) I hold it my boun-den duty to preſent theſe firſt fruits of my labours to your Honour, as an unfayned teſtimony, and an undoubted evidence of my faithfull obſervance, and ſingular reſpect to your Lordſhip : which if you ſhall be pleaſed to take into your ſpecial Patronage and protection, I ſhall be in good hope to be freed both from the venomous tooth of *Momus*, and from the malevolent aſpect of *Zoilus*, and from the poyſoned breath and ſtinging of the reſt of that vi-perous brood, and ſhall alwaies remaine

Your Honours in all dutifull obſervance,

IOHN BABINGTON.

TO
THE READER.

Courteous Reader,

Aving for mine owne private recreati-
on, spent some vacant houres in the
study and contemplation of those ar-
tificiall Fire-works which are dis-
coursed of in the ensuing Treatise; I
held it requisite for my further and better satisfacti-
on, as any opportunity did offer it selfe, to make expe-
riment of some of the particularities there set downe;
and I did accordingly now and then bring into Act
that whereof before I had but a meere Notion, and
the bare and naked Theorie: which because it could
not be done so privately, but that of necessity sometimes
it would come to the view of others; by that meanes it
is come to passe, that more notice than I was ever wil-
ling to, hath beene taken, that I have bestowed some
thoughts upon that subiect, and taken more than ordinary paines in it. And not so onely, but thereupon also
some of my intimate friends and acquaintance, who
have a speciall intrest in me, have beene very instant
and urgent with me that I would make my labours
more publike, and communicate them to the world, by
committing them to the Presse: whereto though I was

a long while utterly unwilling, as being conscious to my selfe of mine owne inability and insufficiency to devise and contrive any thing worthy to come to such publike view, yet their importunity hath at last so farre prevailed with me, that those rude and unpolished lines are now like to see the Sunne, and to come abroad to be scanned and censured by others. If thou shalt looke upon them with a faire and favourable eye, I shall bee encouraged to bestow my paines upon some other thing, which may happily give thee more content, and in the meane while shall rest

Thy true friend and well-willer,

IOHN BABINGTON, Gunner.

In laudem Authoris IOANNIS BABINGTON
Amici & in Arte Mathesios
celeberrima Socii.

THe pleasant object of close ardent Bowres,
Envelloped with *Florae's* fragrant flowres,
The goodly Prospect of Skie-kissing Hils,
Or fertile Plaines vein'd ore with purling Rils:
More ravish not my sences with delight,
Then doth thy *Pyrotechnie.* Many write
Of Arts in themselves worthy, but their worth
Is much impairde by those that set them forth,
Wholly unskill'd in *Megathologie,*
The very soule of each deepe Mysterie.
I wish such shallow men would meddle lesse,
And with their senselesse stuffe not cloy the Presse.
All such his Schoole to passe by *Plato* wilde
In beautifull Geometrie not skild.
Well hast thou then my Friend exprest thy Art,
Since this rare Science hath the greater part
Shar'd in thy Worke, giving it winged fire,
To mount it up-aloft, and deck the ayre
With splendent stars, silver and golden showers;
These are th'effects of *Mathematick* powers:
Which crown their *Authors* temples, not with bayes,
But with a wreath of stars and fulgent rayes.
Fairly goe on, thy selfe such *Trophies* reare,
That neither *Time* nor *Envie* may outweare.

Tho: Stutevill. Philomathes.

Vnto his worthy Friend, and induſtrious Artiſt,
Maſter IOHN BABINGTON.

VVHen as I did thy Booke by chance eſpie,
  With divers figures grac't, moſt curiouſly
  Contriu'd, all new, and of thine own invention,
With ſundry Engines made by iuſt proportion :
I did admire thy skill, thy active braine,
Whereby thoſe things thou didſt ſo well attaine :
Juſtly I might, for of no Nation yet,
There's any bath this path ſo fully beat ;
Nor laid thoſe grounds that thou haſt done, whereby
We might attaine to things that tend ſo high.
For ſenceleſſe things with life thou ſeem'ſt to fill,
Making them wondred at by common skill.
Thou ſundry doubts unfold'ſt, and with much eaſe,
Thou teacheſt us to meaſure Land and Seas.
When as I thought on theſe, and knew how rare
Men thus addicted, and thus given were,
My mind, my hand, my hand did force my pen,
T' offer my mite of thankes 'mongſt other men.
Accept it then, and let it no leſſe bee
Pleaſing, then greater gifts are unto thee.

Thy truly affectionate, and wel-

wiſhing Friend,

John Bate.

In commendations of his worthy Friend Master *John Babington* Gentleman.

I f I were worthy to extoll the Name
O f him that spends the 'Elixer of his spirits,
H ow rare definde, I should set forth the same,
N ere should I flinch; for why thy great demerits
B ravely should arme me boldly to oppose
A gainst thy Criticks and back-biting foes,
B rave man of worth proceed: the rarest wits,
I f thy rare Worke doe come but in their view,
N ere doubt, but they as soone as God permits,
G reat love and aid will then expresse to you,
T hat spends your time, spirits, and great expence
O n Countries good for love, not recompence.
N ow tell me thou that hast a Tallent lent,
Which was receiv'd from *God Omnipotent*,
And hor'dst it up, burying it with thy Name,
It there takes Period, ending with thy frame.
When this my Authors fame, I iust presage,
Shall flourish still), and not weare out with age.

Thy Friend I o h n H i c k s, *alias*

Bridghampton Gunner.

A Table of the Contents.

A Treatise of ARTIFICIALL FIRE-WORKS,
most of them being invented and approved by the Author.

CHAPTER I.

*How to make all sorts of moulds, in a true proportion,
with the Rowlers and Drifts.*

 Hat I may set downe the true proceeding in Fireworkes, it is requisite in the first place to lay downe the true order and forme of making all sorts of moulds, aswell greater as lesse : and to proceed, you must get of the best drie Box you can finde ; if not, of some other tough wood, as Crabbe-tree, Holly, or such like wood, which when you have provided according to your size you meane to use , it behoveth in the next place to be known, of what diameter you will have the heighth of your bore, and from thence all the rest is derived : For example, I desire to have one bored of an inch high, which I get bored by some Turner ; and to know of what length it must be, I take for the sayd length six diameters of the bore, which maketh six inches, and for the thicknesse it ought to be halfe a diameter on each side, so that being turned true round, it contaynes two inches in diameter. Then have you to provide a bottome, which is to be fitted in such sort as you see described in this figure : the proportions heerafter follow.

A *is the foot of the mould, and is in heighth two diameters, which must bee two inches ; and one diameter and $\frac{1}{2}$ in breadth, whether it bee square or round.*

B *serveth only for a stay, and must arise one inch into the mould, which is one diameter, and so proportionall in all other sorts.*

C *is for the mouth of the rocket, and is in diameter $\frac{2}{3}$ of the bore ; so setting one foot of the compasse in the center, describe the arch, which is the full heighth required.*

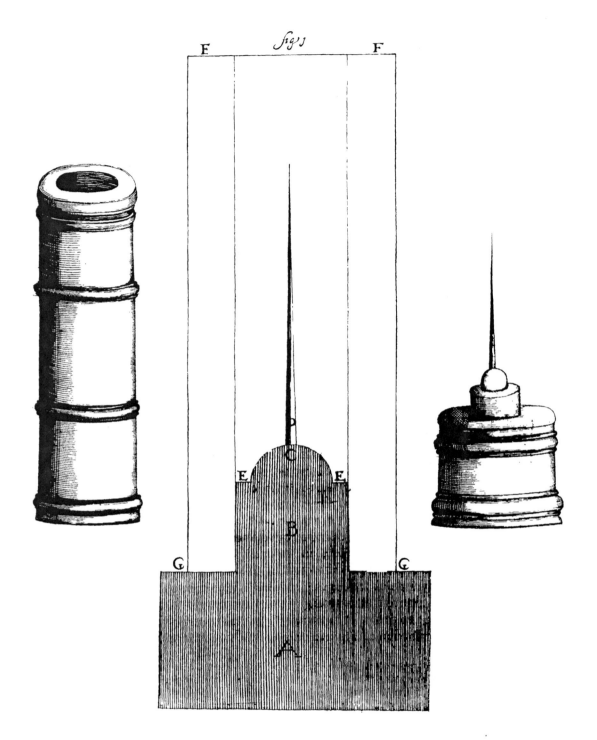

fig. 1

E E ſerveth for the paper being rowled, and is ⅙ part of the diameter on each ſide.

F F is the thickneſſe of the mould, which is halfe the diameter of the bore, that is in this place halfe an inch.

F G the length of the mould, which is ſix diameters.

D the length and bigneſſe of the needle, which is ⅔ the length of the mould, and bigneſſe to be ⅛ of the diameter of the bore at the bottom, and ſow taper to the top.

When you have provided your mould according to your deſire, then you are to fit your rowler, which muſt be two third parts of the diameter of the bore of the ſayd mould, and the length thereof to bee ſix inches longer than your mould, which is for the roling of your paper, and is deſcribed by the letter A in this ſecond figure, with a hole to be bored in the bottom to receive a wyer, which muſt bee faſtned in another peece of wood ſomewhat ſhorter, which is to take out at pleaſure, as you may ſee deſcribed by the letter D : there is required no proportion of length for this ſhort peece ; only it ſufficeth if it be but ſo long as a man may well hold it in his hand ; the uſe hereafter ſhall be more plainly deſcribed when I come to ſpeake of the order of making the coffins ; which ſhall be in the next Chapter. When you have fitted your rocket according to this direction, proceed to the making of your rammers, (or more properly called drifts) which muſt bee alwayes two at the leaſt to, each mould, and as your mould increaſes in largeneſſe, ſo muſt you have more rammers, by reaſon of the largeneſſe of the taper needle : the manner and form you may ſee deſcribed by the letters B C.

B is the hollow rammer, and hath a hole in it anſwerable to the length and bigneſſe of the taper needle, as appeareth in that figure. It muſt be a ſmall matter leſſe than the rowler, becauſe that otherwiſe in putting it in, you will put down the paper, which is very prejudiciall to your rocket.

The other rammer is not halfe ſo long, and is ſad, that when you have beaten to the top of the needle, you make uſe of it : it is deſcribed by the letter C.

When you have fitted your rammers, you muſt provide a peece of Box made after the form as you ſee deſcribed ; which muſt ſerve to make your large coffins to put the work which you intend, on the head of your rockets. It is deſcribed by the letter P, as in the figure is manifeſt.

The letters E E ſhew the diameter, which is the juſt bigneſſe of your rocket, and muſt be ſo in all ſizes.

G G ſhewes the largeneſſe of the coffin, and muſt bee two diameters, which in this figure is two inches.

H H H H ſhewes the length of the coffin, which ought to bee two diameters of your rocket, which in this place is two inches ; but we are not tied to that ſo preciſely; for we are to alter that according to the works which we put therein.

Chap. II.

How to make your coffins of paper.

OW having explained the manner and forme of the moulds, with the rest of the dependants, I come now to shew the use of them in their severall orders: and first for the use of the rowler, which is described by the letter A.

You must provide some good strong paper, as old Law books, which are both strong and large; and cut out your sizes of paper for your work: now to know what length your paper must bee, let it bee alwayes the length of your mould : so shall you have one diameter left above the mould, the use whereof shall be shewn in his proper place. Now having provided your paper in length ready, take your rowler, and one length of paper, and begin to rowle; when you have rowled one sheet, you *Figure 2. G.* must have a board to rowle it with (the board is marked in the second figure;) which must be done in this manner : you must hold the rowler in your left hand, and with your right hold the board; then lay down your rowler upon some smooth chest, or table, or such like; which when you have done, lay on your board, and rowle it very hard, only one way ; which having done, rowle another length, and so proceed in rowling between every sheet, till you have rowled on so much as will fill the mould very straight ; when you have so done, draw forth your rowler one diameter, which in this place is one inch ; and then take the other part of the rowler, which is short, and marked with D, and put it in as you see described ; and there have you a place left for the choaking of your rocket, of which we come now to speak:

Chap. III.

How you shall choak a rocket.

Hen you come to choak your rocket, you must have a ring to screw into some post, at which you must tie your cord, which must be bigger or lesser, according to the bignesse of your rocket, by reason that a small cord will not choak a great rocket for want of strength ; and again, a great cord will not serve for a small, in regard that it will make too great a choaking; so that you must have a bigger and lesse ; which when you have so provided, tying one end to the ring, you must about a yard off tie a stick, in fashion of a handle for a swing, which must bee strong, by reason that it must beare the whole weight of the body, (the letter G in the *Figure 2. K.* second figure expresseth the same ;) which when you have provided,

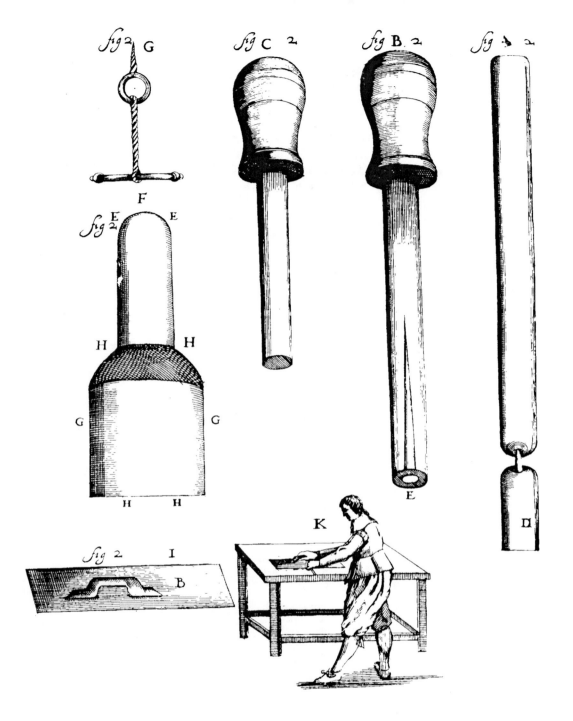

fig 2 G

fig C 2

fig B 2

fig A 2

F

fig E 2
E   E

H   H

G   G

H   H

E

fig 2   I

B

K

Ⅱ

put the sticke betweene your legges, and winde the cord about the rocket case in the place appointed, which is betweene the long rowler and
the short, when you have so done, girt it by degrees, ever turning your
rouler, to the end it may come together more close and neat (the manner is expressed in the third figure, by the letter K) so when you have
choaked it sufficiently, draw forth your short rowler, and where your
choaking is, tye it about with strong packthred; and so drawing forth
your rowler, you have a coffin ready to be filled when occasion serveth,
the forme whereof followeth. And because the choaking of a rocket is
very laborious and dangerous, in regard of the breaking of the cord,
which often hapneth; I haue therefore invented a certaine Engine, wher-
by a childe may choake the strongest rocket. The parts of it are a screw
moving a wheele, on the axeltree of which is fastened your cord for
choaking, with the other end of the cord fastened to a staple on the same
boord: the forme whereof you shall finde described in the third figure,
by the letter B. C.

Figure 3.
K.

Figure 3.
B. C.

Figure 3.

A *Is the coffin of a Rocket wholly finished, with his choaking.*
B *The forme of an Engine for choaking a Rocket.*
C *The mannner of using the Engine.*
F *Is a measure made of horne or latten.*
G *Is a funnell with a handle to fill small Rockets, and other small works.*
H *Is a fine searce, with a receiver to searce your ingredients.*
I *Is a morter to meale your powder, and your other ingredients, which must be of wood, with a pestle.*

Having described the order and formes of all things necessary to the
making of a rocket, it resteth now that we know the manner of driving
it, as also what ingredients are most proper for every size.

Chap. IV.

The manner of driving a Rocket, with the instruments belonging to the same.

Hen you have finished your coffin of paper, take it,
and with your hollow rammer force it downe close
into your mould, which when you have done, strike
two or three smart blowes to settle the paper into his
right forme: which being done, you must begin to
fill your coffin, in doing whereof, you must have a
great care, alwaies providing a measure, which may
containe $\frac{1}{20}$ part of your whole Rocket; so by that meanes you shall not
faile, but every Rocket shall have a true proportion alike; as for Example,
I have a coffin, which being filled, will hold an ounce of mixture or ther-
abouts. I take the twentieth part, and when I finde what quantity it is,
I make a measure of horne, which shall containe so much, and then I
beginne to fill my coffin with one measure at a time, and putting in my
ram-

rammer, ftrike foure or five fmart blowes with a good ftrong mallet, and *Figure* 3. M.
then I fill another meafure, and ftrike againe, fo I continue till I come to
the top of the needle, then I take the fad rammer, and fo continue with it,
till I come to the top of the mould : now the paper which is above the
top of the mould, muft be turned downe, and beaten hard down, which
being done, the Rocket is finifhed from the mould; which force out, with
as much eafe as you can, for the leffe you force it (being filled, and the
needle taken out) the better it is, for knocking loofens the powder, and
fo caufes the Rocket to faile: now it refts to know the receits proper for
every fort of Rockets.

And firft for Rockets of one ounce, you may take only powder duft, being ve- *The ingredi-*
ry fine fearced; which rifes very fwift, but carries no taile of fire with it, and *ents for ordi-*
often times breakes, unleffe they be very thicke of paper : but the beft and fu- *nary Rockets.*
reft way is, to allay your powder with coale duft being well fearced, which cau-
fes a more glorious fhew; and you may ufe it at your difcretion. The ordinary
allay for fmall Rockets is, 1 l. of powder, two ℥. of coaleduft, which ferves till
you come to Rockets of foure ounces, then muft you take to every 1 l. of powder
2½ ℥ of coleduft, continuing that quantity till you come to Rockets of tenne
ounces, and from tenne to fixteene ounces, which is one pound: your allay muft
be to one pound of powder, three ounces of coale.

Now when you have provided your powder, you muft firft meale it,
and then fearce it, fo that it may be free from any corne though never fo
fmall. Likewife take good dry coale, well burnt, and beat it to duft,
fearcing it very fine, which when you have done, mixe them according
as your occafion ferveth, and as your directions are.

Chap. V.

The manner of heading a Rocket, with the order of capping it.

Ow we come to fhew the manner of heading a Rocket, in which we are to ufe our thicke Roler, fpecifi-
ed in the fecond figure, and marked with F. Vpon
which you muft role fome paper or fine paft-board,
and paft it fo that it may bee very clofe, and then
choake it at the length of the thicker part, fo that it
may come clofe to your fticke in the leffer part,
which will fit to be tyed to the top of your Rocket,
fo fhall you have a coffine to put in your workes, which muft bee of divers forts. That being done, you muft provide Taper caps, which muft
be adjoyned to the top of the large coffin. The ufe of them is to keepe in
your workes, and to caufe them to pierce the ayre more fwiftly: The
manner of making thefe caps, is, to take a paire of Compaffes, and defcribe
a circle in paftboard, then cut it forth with a paire of fheeres, and that
fhall make two cappes, being cut in the middle, and turned one corner
under the other, and fo pafted; and let them fo pafted, be put in a napkin
preffe,

preſſe till they be dry, and when they be dry, cut out a ſemicircle in paper, which ſhall fit round about the ſaid cap, and ſhall ſerve to paſte on the cap to the coffin: the forme whereof is expreſſed in the fourth figure, by the figure 14. and 15. ſo have you all things ready to the finiſhing of your Rocket, which muſt be done as followeth.

Chap. 6.

The manner of finiſhing a Rocket.

 Hen your Rocket is driuen, as I have ſhewed you, with the paper turned downe, you ſhall firſt prime it, which muſt be with cotton wicke made for the ſaid purpoſe, which you ſhall put up into the vent, leaving a peece to hang lower than the mouth of your Rocket, by three or foure inches, which being done, tye a piece of paper over the mouth, to the end it fall not out: now having primed your Rocket, you may proceede to the heading of it, and that is done after this manner. Take your Rocket, and on the head (where I told you, you ſhould turne downe the paper, you muſt with a bodkin, pierce two or three holes, to the intent that the Rocket having ſpent himſelfe, your workes which are on his head, may take fire; which holes, prime with a little powder duſt, and then put on his head, with the choaking fitted to your Rocket, which muſt come over the Rocket, in ſuch manner, that the bottome of the greater part muſt come even with the top of the Rocket; which tye faſt to your rocket with threed, and then put in your workes: but before you put in your workes, whether they be ſtarres, or any other workes, you muſt put in a little cotton wooll, being rowled in powder duſt, to the end your ſtars may fire, and likewiſe may blow out : which having done, put in your ſtarres, or other workes, and if you make more than one tire (as you may doe of your ſtarres) then muſt you put more cotton rowled in powder duſt amongſt them, or betweene every tire, to the end they may all take fire; then take your cap ſo provided as I have formerly ſhewed, and fill the hollow place with cotton, becauſe it is light, and likewiſe will fire quickly: which being fitted, paſte it cloſe to the top of the coffin, in ſuch manner, that it may ſtand very upright; then muſt you fit on your ſticke, for the peaſing of your Rocket, which ought to be about eight lengths of your Rocket without the head. You muſt get the ſmootheſt and lighteſt you can, ſuch as baſket makers uſe; which when you have got, you muſt make very ſtrait, and then cutting one ſide of it, flat at the great end, make two notches on the round ſide, provided that the one be differing from the other, ſo much as is betweene the choaking of your Rocket, and the end of the vent; becauſe if you ſhould tye it upon the vent, it would looſen the powder, and ſo cauſe it to breake in the firing. Now that you tye not the wrong end of your
Rocket

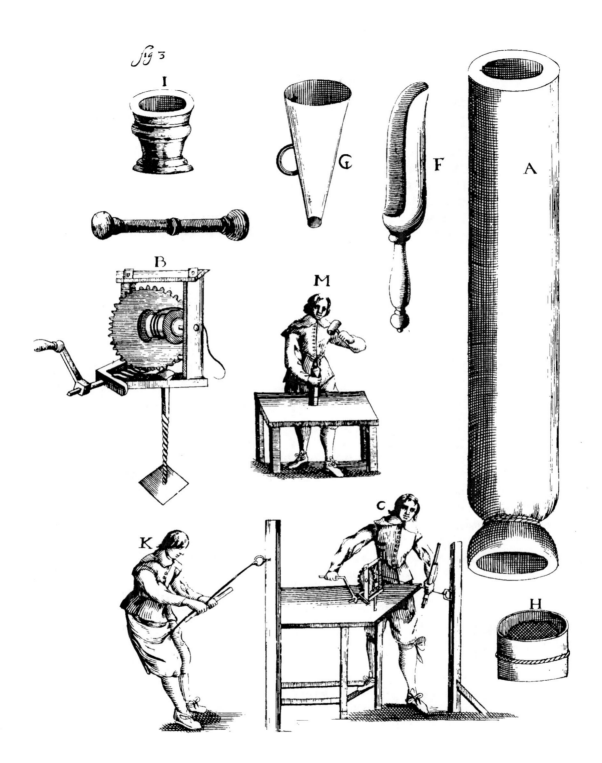

Rocket uppermost, as some foolishly have done, for want of better instructions, you must alwayes tye the end downewards, which is choaked, and with a piece of strong thred tye it fast to the lower notch, just about the choaking, so shall you be sure your stickes shall not fall off, neither will it indanger the hurting of your rocket. When you have tyed that, then proceed to the tying of it higher, which as I say, must be somewhat higher than the top of the vent, and let your sticke come even with the top of your rocket; which having done, pease your rocket, which must be after this manner. Lay it on your finger two or three inches or more from the mouth, and if you finde the stick be too heavy, cut it shorter, till you finde your Rocket to ballance your sticke, for the sticke being too heavy, causes your rocket to slugge, and being too light, it makes a rocket fall before he is halfe up : these things being provided, you have your rocket ready to be fired, which must be after this manner.

CHAP. VII.

The manner of firing Rockets, with the description of a
staffe for the firing of them.

Rovide a long staffe with a pike at one end, which must be thrust hard into the ground, and a three legged staffe with a hollow hoope at the top, to let this long staffe slide up and downe, to the end that having rockets, whose stickes are longer than your said staffe, yet by raising it through the said iron hoope, you may make it foure or five foot longer than it would be standing on the ground. Now this long staffe must have a sliding peece cut with severall points, which must be neere the top; and at the bottome there must be a ring of wyer, to let the sticke goe through, which must be made likewise to slide up and downe; so thrusting the small end through the said ring, your rocket will rest upon that part above, which must be just opposite in a straight line, so open the mouth of your rocket, and pull out the end of your cotton wicke, and with a peece of match, fastened in a Linstocke, give fire to the said wicke, and by degreees, you shall see it fire your rocket; which being well ordered, will mount very straight and high : now having shewed the whole order of composing a rocket, with the firing of the same, I will shew you an order for making of your starres, and other workes which are necessary for the heads of your rockets; and first of all I will shew you the making of divers sorts of starres, with their compositions; and since wee cannot make them without the compositions, I will first set downe the compositions, and then proceed to the manner of making them.

CHAP.

Chap. VIII.
Divers Compofitions for ſtarres.

A Compoſition for ſtarres of a blew colour, with red.

ſAke of powder mealed,	8 ℥
Salt peter,	4 ℥
Sulphur vive,	12 ℥

Meale theſe very fine, and mixe them together with 2 ℥. of aqua vite, and ⅓ ℥. of oyle of ſpicke, which let be very dry before you uſe it.

Another Compoſition which maketh a white fire and beautifull.

Take powder,	4 ℥
Salt peter,	12 ℥
Sulphur vive,	6 ℥
Camphire,	½ ℥

Meale your ingredients, and mixe them; now to powder your Camphire, you muſt dip your peſtle in oyle of Almonds, or ſuch like oyle : you muſt not uſe your wooded peſtle for this, becauſe that oyle will ſoake into it, which is an enemy to ſome workes; therefore take a braſſe peſtle and morter, and dipping the peſtle in oyle of Almonds, put it to your Camphire, and ſo ſtirring it by degrees, it will powder; which when you have done, keepe it very cloſe from ayre, till ſuch time as you uſe it, otherwiſe the Camphire will loſe his ſpirit, and become of no uſe.

Another white fire which laſteth long.

Take powder,	4 ℥
Salt peter,	1 ℔
Sulphur vive,	8 ℥
Camphur,	1 ℥
Oyle of peeter,	2

Meale thoſe which are to be mealed, very fine, and mixe them according to the former directions:

CHAP.

CHAP. IX.

The manner of making the best sort of starres.

Now having set downe the compositions for starres, it resteth to know how these starres are made, which is divers waies, but I will set you downe onely two waies both which are very good, so that you may take your choyce. The first is this, you must make little square pieces of browne paper, which fill with your composition *Figure 4.* you intend, and so double it downe, rolling it till you make it somewhat *N. G.* round, about the bignesse of a nut or bigger, according to the size of your rocket; you may put in a dozen on the head of a small rocket; when you have made them up in this forme, you must binde them round with small thred, which done, draw through a cotton wicke prepared for priming, as hereafter shall be shewne.

The second sort are made after another manner, which is thus; you must have a rowler, as big as an ordinary arrow, which shall be to rowle a length of paper about it, and with a little mouth glue, or paste, paste it round; so have you a hollow trunke of paper, which you shall order after this manner: Fill it by little and little with your small funnell, still thrusting it very hard, till you have filled it to the top; which done, cut it into short pieces, about halfe an inch in length; then having in readinesse either hot glue, or size mingled with red lead, dip one end of your short pieces, to the end, that both ends of your starre fire not, and also that it may not blow out; which being so finished, set to dry till you use them, and then putting the other end into powder dust, you may put them on your rocket, in one or two tier; alwaies provided, as I said before, that you put in powder dust betweene every tier, to the end they may all fire; thus have you the manner of making your starres, the formes whereof you shall have described hereafter.

Priming for   The priming before spoken of, is made after this manner; take oyle of *Rockets.* Camphire, and soake some cotton wicke in it, then take it out being moyst, and rowle it in fine powder dust, which having done, you shall hang it up till it be thorow dry, so have you prepared a very good priming, which must be kept close from ayre, till such time you have occasion, otherwise the spirit of the Camphir will decay.

The description of the staffe for firing of Rockets.

A *The long staffe to rise through the ring.*
B B B *The three legd staffe.*
C *The ring or hoope of iron for the long staffe to slide thorow.*
D *A screw to screw fast the long staffe being raised.*
E *A piece of iron filed with notches to hang the Rockets on.*
F *The ring of wyer to put thorow the sticke, which may be raised higher, put lower, as occasion proffers.*
G G *The description of two starres, with the priming,* K, *and the binding* L.
H *The description of the trunke, or case, which is to be filled with your star mixture, and so cut into short pieces, as you see represented by the figures* I. I.
where

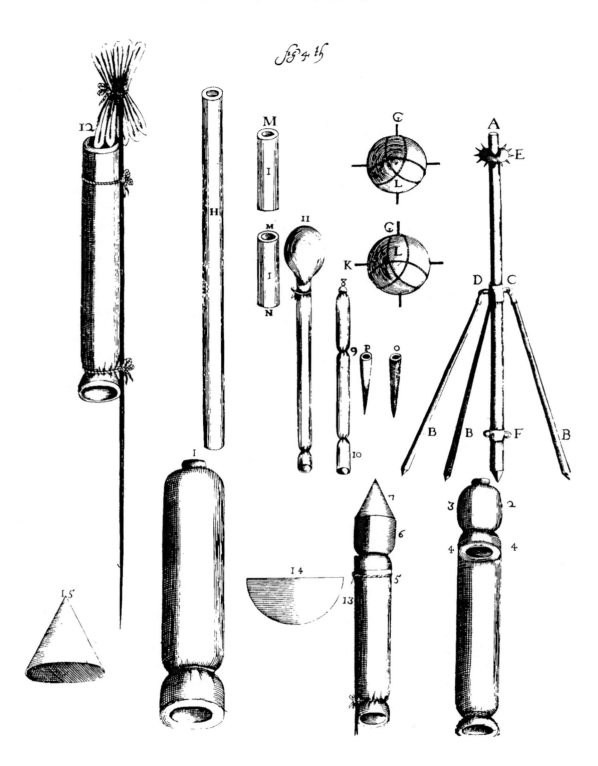

fig 4 th

where the vper part reprefents the open end, and is marked with M, *and the vnder part which is glued, is reprefented by the letter* N, *fo have you the ftarres wholly defcribed.*

CHAP: X.

The manner of making filver and gold raine.

Ow I will fhew you the order for making of golden raine, which is after this manner; you muſt prouide ſtore of Gooſe quils, which hauing, you muſt cut off the quill as long as you can leaue it, and cut not off the other end, but leaue it cloſe as you ſee preſented by the letters O P. Figure 4. where O reprefents one filled, and P one empty. The receit which you make your golden raine, muſt be the ſame which you make your rockets of one ounce, which is to 1 l. of powder, 2 ℈. of coaleduſt: now hauing filled many of theſe quils, as I haue ſhewed you, they muſt be put on the head of your rocket, with the open ends downward, to the end they may take fire fo ſoone as your rocket is ſpent, and fo ſhall you ſee appeare a ſhower of gold, which by ſome is called golden raine: the like way may you make ſiluer raine, filling your quils with the mixture prefcribed for your white ſtarres, and uſing them in the ſame manner, you ſhall ſee them fall downe like a ſhower of ſiluer, which is called ſiluer raine; and thus much ſhall ſuffice to be knowne for this ſort of worke.

CHAP. XI.

How to make Fiſgigs, which ſome call Serpents.

Ow I will fhew you to make another ſort of work, which we call Fiſgigs, or as the French name them, Serpents, which are made as followeth. You muſt prouide a ſmall mould, of ⅓ of an inch diameter, which muſt bee made without a needle, which when you have, you muſt make your caſes, as you make for your rockets, choaking them ⅓ an inch from the end, which ſhall ſerue for occaſion as it ſhall bee proffered; when you haue made your caſes, fill them three inches with powder duſt, and then choake him, and after put in a little corne powder, to the end that your Fiſgig hauing plaied a while to and fro, hee may breake and giue a report; the uſe of the making fo deepe a mouth at your firſt choaking is, that you may fill it with your ſtarre mixture; fo that putting diuers of them on the head of a large rocket, they will firſt appeare like fo many ſtarres, and when the ſtarres are ſpent, taking hold of the powder duſt, they will run wrigling to and fro like Serpents, and after a while they will giue fo many reports, which will giue great content.

There

There are many works which are made of thefe fisgigs, which wee will fpeak of in their places.

CHAP. XII.

How to make the reports or breakers.

OW I will proceed to fhew the manner of making reports to place on the head of a rocket ; you muft make a coffin of the fize of your rocket of one inch, but you muft rowle your paper a great deale thicker, to the intent your report may be the greater;alfo in choaking,the mouth muft bee left very large, to the end that on occafion you may fill it with ftarre mixture ; now when you have made divers coffins about three inches and better in length, you muft leave a fmall vent at the choaking, the bigneffe of an ordinary wyer, which you muft ftop with a little paper, while you fill the coffin almoft full, or within halfe an inch of the top, with good corn powder, turning down foure or five folds of paper, choak it clofe at the top, and binde it round with thred, fo you have your reports ready, againft fuch time you come to ufe them ; which muft be done in this manner : firft bee carefull to pull out your ftopple, which having done, fill the mouth with your ftarre mixture, and fo faften him on the top of your rocket, alwayes putting a little paper about the top of your rocket, and in it put a little powder duft, and fo fet on your report, and tie it faft on, with the mouth towards the head of the rocket, fo that the rocket having fpent himfelfe, you fhall fee a large ftar appeare,and when it is neere the ground,you fhal heare the report ; the order thereof you fhall finde defcribed in the fourth figure.

   1 *Is the report ready finifhed.*

   2 *The rocket with the report on the head.*

   3 *The report faftned on the head of the rocket.*

   4 *The paper to faften the report to the rocket, which muft firft bee tied to the rocket, and likewife to the report.*

   8 *Reprefenteth a fisgig finifhed.*

   9 *The choaking, as I have fhewed, which muft bee filled upward with corn powder.*

   10 *The mouth of your fisgig, which upon occafion you may fill with your ftarre mixture, to put on the head of your rockets.*

   11 *Reprefenteth a fisgig, with a bladder, which muft be tyed on to the head of them, in fuch manner, that the neck of the bladder may go into the fisgig, and fo be faft tyed, that they ftirre not ; the ufe of them is, only to fire in your hand, (for being fired with a little powder duft in the mouth of it) and fo caft away from you, it will fly to and fro without ceafing, till it hath fpent it felfe ; and by reafon of the bladder which is tied to it, it will not ftick faft to the ground, as others do which have no bladders.*

   12 *Reprefenteth a cracker faftned to the top of a rocket, fo that the rocket having fpent himfelfe, it taketh fire, and maketh many reports ; the manner*

of

of faſtning him is thus ; you muſt firſt tie on your rocket, leaving the ſtick ſo much higher than the top, as will ſuffice to tie on your cracker, which muſt be tied about the ſaid ſtick, in ſuch manner, that the noſe of it may come into the head of your rocket; which being primed with ſome powder duſt, will take fire.

5 Repreſenteth a rocket with ſeverall works, whether ſtarres, or ſerpents, and muſt be with a large coffin on the top, with his cap.

6 Is the coffin, which as I have ſhewed you, muſt bee ſomewhat bigger than your rocket.

7 Is the cap, which muſt be taper.

13 Sheweth the faſtning of the ſtick, which muſt not bee higher than your rocket, beſide the large coffin.

All which I have formerly deſcribed, with the form and manner of making them, and their ſeverall uſes ; ſo that I have fully layd down the whole order of finiſhing a rocket for the ayre. Now it reſteth to ſhew what other works may bee done by the ſayd rockets, which are many ; for all ſorts of Fire works for pleaſure, do wholly depend upon them, except the water bals : and to proceed, I will firſt deſcribe unto you the order of making the runners on the line, which muſt bee done in manner following.

CHAP. XIII.

How to make a runner on the line.

OV muſt provide a ſmall rocket mould, which muſt be halfe an inch or more, with rowlers, and rammers, according as I have deſcribed, ſave only that your mould muſt have no needle, nor your rammers hollow ; when you have provided them, make up your caſes, after the form which I have ſhewed you, ſome longer, and ſome ſhorter, which muſt be uſed as followeth ; your ſhort ones muſt be beaten up to the top, which muſt not bee above foure inches ; your longer, which muſt bee 5 ½ inches, muſt bee likewiſe filled foure inches high, and the reſt to be filled with corn powder within halfe an inch of the top, which muſt be choaked cloſe, and tied up ; the receipt for theſe ſorts muſt be only fine powder duſt.

Receipt for runners.

Now when you have driven them as is ſhewed, you may proceed to the finiſhing of them, which muſt be in this manner ; you muſt rowle a peece of paper about the head of your ſhorter rocket, (which muſt be left open to give fire to the next) which paper muſt be five inches broad, and being rowled on, you muſt firſt try if the mouth of your other rocket will eaſily go in, which when you have done, draw forth your other rocket which you tried, and binde your paper faſt to the top of your ſhort one, in ſuch manner, that foure inches may remaine hollow above the top of your rocket, which is to be filled with powder duſt, about two

inches

inches high ; then put in your longer rocket, (with the mouth inward) so farre as it may touch your powder duſt ; and tie the paper faſt about the choaking, as you ſhall finde deſcribed in the fift figure ; after you have done this, proceed to the putting on of your cane, which muſt bee after this manner ; you muſt firſt provide canes of ſuch bigneſſe as will fit your line, and cut them three inches long, or ſomewhat better, and then notch them with three notches, which when you have ſo provided, firſt tie it to your longer rocket which is to fire laſt, and then doubling them together, (in ſuch ſort that the noſe of the firſt come farther out than the tayle of the ſecond) tie it to them both ; the reaſon of this is, becauſe otherwiſe, if it were tied to them both together, and not to one ſeverally, ſo ſoon as the firſt were fired, the cane will grow ſlack, and often fall off, and never make his returne ; and againe, if you ſhould not put the mouth of the one farther out than the tayle of other, it would fire your other rocket, and ſo make a confuſion : therefore that you may the better un-derſtand what I have ſhewed you, I have ſet down in this fift figure, the whole order of finiſhing a runner for the line.

A *Is the ſhort rocket.*
B *Is the longer, which muſt be beaten foure inches with powder duſt, and one inch with corn powder.*
C C *Your two rockets joyned, the mouth of one to the tayle of the other, in ſuch ſort, that there may be two inches between them.*
D *The coffin of paper which joynes thoſe two together, and muſt bee filled with powder duſt, lightly put in.*
E E *The rockets doubled, with the cane tied on.*
F *The cane, which muſt be three inches long, or more.*
G *The cord that paſſeth thorow the cane.*
H *A peece of cork on the end of the line.*

CHAP. XIV.

The manner of firing your runner.

NOW having thus finiſhed your runners, you muſt pro-vide a line, which may bee a hundred yards, or more, as your ground will permit, ſo faſtning your cord at the fartheſt of your diſtance, provide a peece of board or cork, with a hole of the bigneſſe of your line, which muſt bee put on the end of your line, to the end that your rocket may not reſt againſt any thing that may hinder it in the re-trogade motion ; alwayes provided, you ſope your line very well, for feare of firing : then put on your runner at the other end (with the mouth of the rocket towards you, which muſt bee primed with powder duſt) and pull your line very ſtraight, which is a great help to the running of a rocket, ſo faſtning your cord, you may fire your runner, which being well ordered, will run to the fartheſt of your line, making his returne, with a report at laſt ; ſo have you finiſhed the runner.

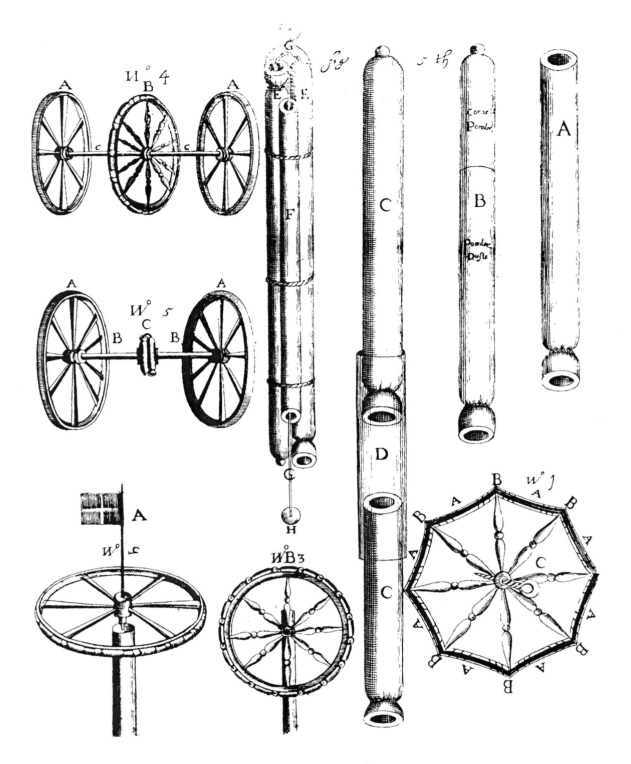

CHAP. XV.

How to compose a wheele.

OW I will shew you the order of composing a wheele, which is a prime work, being well ordered ; of which some are movable, and some immovable : of the movable, some move horizontall, and some verticall, which is toward the zenith: and first of the movable wheele.

You must provide a wheele of such diameter as you please, which must be made into squares, according to the circumference of your wheele, and to proportion your wheele into a just number, you may allow five inches or better for every side, so that your wheele being 14 inches diameter, the circumference will be as 7 to 22, which is 44 inches circumference ; so being divided by 5, there will bee 8 squares, or more properly, 8 sides, which will every one containe 5 inches and $\frac{4}{10}$, which is the cord of 45 degrees ; these sides must bee hollowed with a groofe fitting your rockets, and at the ends of every side it must bee filed with notches, to fasten your binding that it slide not, when you binde fast your rockets ; the form whereof you shall finde in the fift figure N 1.

Figure 5.
N 1.

A *Sheweth the 8 sides.*
B *The places of fastning.*
C *The screw which fastneth the wheele to some post.*

Note alwayes, that as your wheele doth increase in diameter, so you must increase in the proportion, for that rocket which forces about a wheele of 14 inches, will not force a wheele of 18 inches ; nor that rocket which forceth one of 18 inches, will not force one of 24 inches ; but that you may come to a neere proportion, I will satisfie you so neere as I can ; first seek the diameter of your wheele, which imagine to bee 18 inches, I take the third thereof, which is 6, so that your rocket for 18 inches diameter, must be 6 inches long, and your wheele of 24 inches diameter, will require rockets of 8 inches ; yet as your wheele encreaseth, you may alter this proportion by dividing it into more sides.

Now having provided your wheele, with your rockets of a just size, you shall proceed to the finishing of it, which must bee after this manner ; you must joine your rockets one to another, in such sort as I shewed you for your runners, that is, with the mouth of the one to the top of the other, and so proceed till you have fastned so many as will serve your wheele, alwayes leaving so much space between each rocket, as may suffer them to come round about your wheele, without breaking any ; which when you have done, proceed to the tying of them on to your wheele, which must be so ordered, that you tie them where the notches are, to the end they faile not in firing, by sliding off. In tying them on you must provide that you leave a little distance between the first and the last, which must be parted with a bolster of paper well soaped, to the end

end that the firft fire not the laft, and fo caufe a great confufion. Now for the manner of placing them, it is according to the workmans pleafure, which muft be either horizontall, or verticall ; for the horizontail wheele you muft provide a poft faftned in the ground, and ſcrew your wheele to the top of it ; for the verticall, you muft ſcrew it on the fide of the poft, fo having fired them, you ſhall fee one run parallell to the horizon, and the other to the zenith, as you ſhall fee defcribed in the fift figure.

N 2 *Reprefenteth the horizontall wheele.*
N 3 *Reprefenteth the verticall wheele.*

There are many other works which do wholly depend upon the wheele, of which I will fet down fome few.

CHAP. XVI.

How to make a ground wheele.

Ere I will declare unto you the manner of making a paire of wheels to run upon a plain horizon ; provide two wheels, (fuch as are ſpinning wheels) of one bigneſſe, which muft bee faftned to a fmall axeltree, in fuch manner, that they may not move about the axeltree, and on the middle of the axeltree faften a fire wheele, which let bee fo much leſſe than the other, that it touch not the ground, fo that being faft upon the fame axeltree, it cannot run unleffe it carry the other with it, which being fet on a plain horizon, will run a great way without ceafing : now that you may make it return, you may provide your wheele in fuch manner, that it may have rockets on both fides, fo that one fide being fpent, it may give fire to the other, which being faftned with their mouthes the contrary way, will make a return with a fwift motion.

The form of thefe ground wheeles you may fee reprefented in the fift figure, N 4.

A A *the two wheeles faftned to the axeltree.*
C C *the axeltree on which the three wheeles are all faftned.*
B *the fire wheele, which is reprefented of a leſſer diameter than the other two.*

CHAP.

CHAP. XVII.

Another manner of ground wheeles.

HEre is another kinde of ground wheeles, and that is made so, that the wheeles may move about the axeltree ; but this sort is not moved about by a wheele, in regard the axeltree muſt ſtand ſtill, but it is made after this manner ; you muſt make your axeltree ſomewhat broad about the midſt of it, and in that place you ſhall boare two holes, into which you ſhall put two rockets, which muſt bee ſo cloſe one to the other, that they may almoſt touch, and muſt bee ſo joined together, that one having ſpent himſelfe, the other may take fire, after the manner of your line work, to the end that being fired, it may run firſt one way, and then the other taking fire, may make his return by a ſecond motion : now the rockets which you put into this place, muſt alwayes bee proportioned according to the bigneſſe of your wheele, which if you perform according to the direction, you ſhall have your deſire.

The form of this wheele is expreſſed in the fiſt figure N 4.

    A A *the two wheeles being looſe upon their axeltree.*
    B B *the axeltree in which the rockets are put.*
    C *the place for the two rockets to be faſtned, which muſt be ſo ordered, that the mouth of one may joyne to the tayle of the other.*

It is eſpecially to be noted, that theſe wheeles muſt run upon a very plain horizon, ſuch as the place for the game of Pall Maile at St. *Iameſes*, or ſome other very ſmooth place ; by reaſon that after the firſt firing of a rocket, his violence is over, and ſo a ſmall thing will ſtay him.

There are alſo ſundry ſorts of wheeles, which do perform divers offices ; ſome for diſplaying of a Coat of Armes, and others for ſetting of divers circular works, ſome of them I will ſpeak of ; and firſt I will ſhew the manner of making a horizontall wheele, which with one firing ſhall give divers reports, and ſhall ſtand fixed.

Снар.

CHAP. XVIII.

The manner of making a fixed wheele, which shall give divers reports.

YOV muſt firſt get a wheele turned by ſome work-man, which muſt be two foot in diameter, (or as you pleaſe to augment or diminiſh your work) which muſt have a grooſe turned out of the upper ſide, of halfe an inch wide, and likewiſe as deep; to which grooſe you muſt have a peece of wood ſo fitted, that it may juſt ſlide in, which peece of wood muſt have ſo many ſmall holes bored in it as you will have reports about it, alwayes provided, you ſet them not too neere together, becauſe the firing of one may not beat down the other ; when you have thus provided your wheele, make a conveyance or hollow trunck of paper which will iuſt fill it, which muſt bee filled with ſome of your ſlow mixtures for ſtarres, and then putting on the cap of wood ſo fitted with holes, and made very faſt with glew, pierce every hole into your hollow conveyance, ſo that putting a quill into eve-ry one, they may take fire, and to the ſaid quill faſten a report, ſo ſhall you have a peale of Chambers placed in a ſmall roome, which being once fired, will follow in order till the whole train be ſpent.   The form you ſhall ſee expreſſed in the ſixt figure marked A.

Figure 6.
A.

CHAP. XIX.

How to make a fixed wheele which ſhall caſt forth many rockets into the ayre.

THere is likewiſe another ſort of wheele not much unlike to the former, which ſhall give fire to divers rockets ſtanding circular, the order differs nothing from the former, only you muſt make a hole for every ſtick to paſſe thorow, and therefore it muſt be made ſomewhat broader, which will effect the ſame as the other doth, by conveying fire from one rocket to another, till they bee all ſpent ; the mix-ture for this conveyance ought to bee very ſlow, wherefore I adviſe you to take this enſuing, which is both ſlow and ſure.

Take Roch peter,   8
Sulphur vive,   4
Camphire,   1½
Fine powder duſt,   2

Mealc

Meale thefe ingredients very fine, and incorporate them, adding $\frac{1}{8}$ $\S$ of Linſeed oyle, and $\frac{1}{8}$ $\S$ of oyle of peter; theſe oyles muſt be dropped in by degrees, and ſo wrought up, till you finde your mixture bound like dough, which if you performe well, will bee both ſlow and ſure. The *Figure 6.* forme of this wheele is expreſſed in the ſixth Figure, by the letter B. B.

Chap. XX.

How to make a fixed wheele, which ſhall caſt forth divers Fiſgigs, and likewiſe as many reports or breakers.

 Auſe a wheele to bee turned, with a grooſe on the top to put in your conveiance of paper; then fit on a peece of wood, as I have formerly ſhewed you, with ſmall holes to put in quils, which are for the firing of your reports, and muſt bee placed round about the uper part of your wheele; and on the ſide thereof, ſhall be made divers holes of the bigneſſe of your Fiſgigs, (which ſhall be ſo pierced thorow to the paper conveiance) thoſe fiſgigs that are placed round on the ſide, & the reports on the top, one traine ſhall fire them all, and in firing, you ſhall ſee all the Fiſgigs flying round about, one after another, as the fire paſſeth to them; and for every Fiſgig which paſſeth out, ſhall bee fired a report, ſo that there ſhall be a continuall motion untill the whole traine bee conſumed: the forme of this wheele is repreſented in the ſixth Figure, by the letter G.

G *Repreſents the wheele finiſhed, with Reports and Fiſgigs.*
R R *Repreſents the reports, placed on the uper part of the wheele.*
F F *Repreſents the Fiſgigs placed round on the ſide of the wheele.*

Chap. XXI.

The manner of making a wheele which ſhall runne two waies, which is, forward and backward.

 Auſe a wheele to be made, ſo that the rockets may be placed on each ſide, with a hole thorow one ſide, which ſhall ſerve for a vent, paſſing from one ſide to the other, then place your rockets firſt upon one ſide, provided that the laſt rocket be placed over the ſaid hole, and boring a ſmall hole in one ſide of that rocket, put in a cotton wicke for priming, and let it come through your wheele, to the mouth of another rocket, which ſhall bee turned the contrary way; ſo that the wheele having finiſhed his revolution one way, may take fire

on

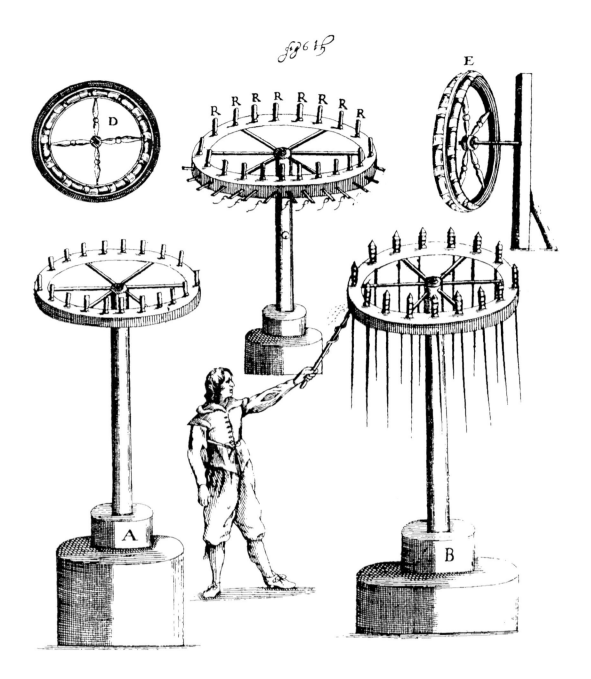

on the other fide, and fo make a retrograde motion : and as you doe this,
fo may you after the fame manner, make a wheele which fhall runne di-
rect, and continue twife fo long as another of the fame bignefse, which
is by placing the rockets the fame way on both fides. The forme of this
is expreffed in the 6 Figure, by the letters D and E.

D *Reprefents the wheele with Rockets placed on the one fide, the laft rockets having a vent, to paffe through to the other fide.*

E *Reprefents the faid wheele finifhed with Rockets on both fides.*

CHAP. XXII.

*The manner of compofing a wheele, which having finifhed his
revolution, fhall reprefent a Coat of Armes.*

 Ake a wheele of fome light board, fo that it may be
without any fpoakes, and upon one fide of it, let
be drawne, that Coat of Armes you intend to reprefent, then boare fo many holes in the wood, as
may conveniently ftand on the traced lines, then
on the other fide, neere the top, fhall a place bee
made, which may containe your rockets, with a
hole pierced thorow where the laft rocket muft
reft. This being done, place your rockets round about, fo that the laft
rocket may be placed on the vent which muft bee primed carefully, to
paffe thorow to the other fide; having placed on the rockets, fill thofe
holes on the other fide with fome flow mixture, fuch as is for your ftars,
or the like, then cover it over with paper, and put in fome powder duft
to fire it, and to break the paper, which being done, fope it well over for
feare of fome fparkes lighting on the paper before the appointed time of
firing, fo have you a wheele ready which you muft put on an axeltree, fo
that it may ftand verticall, and then firing it, you fhall have your de-
fire, for fo foone as the wheele hath fpent his moving worke, it will giue
fire to the other fide; and then ftanding ftill, you fhall fee a perfect Coat
of Armes in fire. Figure 7. A. B.

A *Reprefents that fide of the wheele which hath the Rockets placed on it.*

B *Reprefents the Coat of Armes, in which the round fpots fignifie the places
to be filled with a flow mixture, which muft bee moift, to the end it keepe
clofe in.*

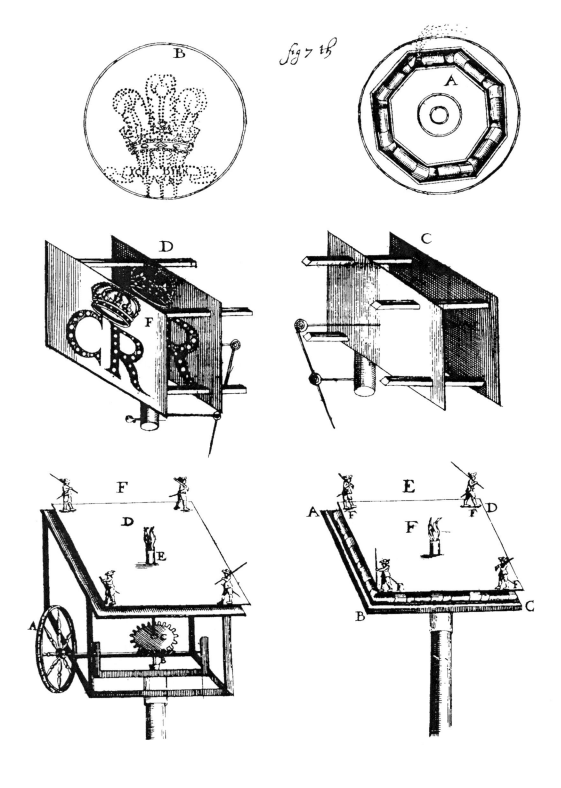

fig 7 th

B

A

D

F

C

F

D

E

F

E

A

F

D

F

B

C

CHAP. XXIII.

*How to reprefent a Coat of Armes in fire, which having burnt a
fmall while, the faid Coat fhall appeare in his perfect colours,
and fhall continue fo a long while.*

 Irft caufe a board to be made foure fquare, of what
dimenfion you pleafe, which let be ¾ an inch thicke,
and caufe a Painter or fome drafts man to trafe out
what Armes or other figure you pleafe, upon the
faid board; alfo let there be another which fhall bee
an inch and ½ thicke, and of the fame breadth, which
faften to the other with fome fmall tackes, till you
have boared fo many holes as you have occafion for,
which fhall behalfe an inch afunder, and likewife halfe an inch boare;
then boare your holes thorow your inch board, and let them enter an
inch into the thicker-planke, then make foure fquare holes (one at each
corner) in the thicker planke, to receive foure fquare pieces of wood,
which muft be an inch fquare, which glue faft into foure holes oppofite
to the other in the thinner planke, to the end it may flide to and fro; then
faften an iron rod in the midft of the thinner, fo that it may come thorow
the thicker planke, and be faftened to a piece of wood, which may turne
upon a joynt; to the end you may draw the thinner fquare neerer as your
fire confumes, and muft draw it too foot at leaft; then provide a fmall arrow of two foot long, and upon it rowle fo much paper, till it fill your
fmall holes exactly, then fill fo many as you have holes already provided
in your fquare, and put them thorow the thinner piece, and the ends
thereof into the thicker, which let be glued faft into the bottome of that,
fo that they may ftand very faft, and likewife let them paffe fo eafily thorow the other holes, that the board may flide nearer or further, to or from
the fire, at pleafure; then fit a piece of paft-board, fo that it may come
clofe about thefe rouled lances, and may fit as exactly as the board doth
at the other end; and let this come within halfe an inch of the firing end,
then prime them all with quicke powder duft, and cover it over with
paper, which having performed, you are ready againft fuch time as you
have occafion to fire it, which muft be after this manner, obferving which
fide the winde is; ftand on that fide, and fire it at the lower corner, fo that
by the helpe of the winde, you fhall have it all fire at once; which having burnt a while, will come to the paft-board and fire it, fo that falling
away, there will be reprefented a Coat of Armes in colours, clofe to your
fire, which may be drawne in by one ftanding behinde, fo that it fhall
feeme alwaies to be ftanding in one place, and the light not to grow
fhorter till the laft. The forme of this frame is prefented in the feventh
figure C D.

A *The frame without the fcutcheon or letters.*
B *The backe fide of the frame, with an iron rod paffing thorow it, and faftened*

to the other part, and the moving part which slideth to and fro as occasion proffers.

D *The frame finished ready to put in your lances.*

F *Represents the face of the frame, or thinner board.*

G *The inner part of the fixed piece, with holes boared in each alike, to put in your lances of rowled paper, filled with slow composition.*

CHAP. XXIV.

How to represent an antike dance, by the helpe of fire, which shall move in a circular forme.

Ause a board to bee made of two foot square, so that one side of it may bee hollowed, (or grooved) to lay your rockets in; then cause another board to bee made of the same largenesse, so that it may sit close on the other, the rockets lying betweene, and in the center of the same board, place a brasse socket, which must passe thorow the other for the center pinne to enter into it; then place your antike figures on the top of the said board, with wiers passing thorow both; to the end they may be turned about in their motion, by certaine pinnes placed in another board, which must stand fixed; so that moving about the said board, the pinnes take hold of the wiers which come thorow, and turne them backward and forward; but in regard of the extraordinary violence of this motion, it will teare all in pieces, unlesse you have a great care in making all things to runne very exactly, which must bee tried before you come to use it. The order of this is represented in the seventh Figure by the letter E.

    A B C D *The bottome board, which stands fixed with a socket to put on a long pole, and hath a small pinne standing at each corner.*

    E E E *The under board which moveth, in which is placed the rockets.*

    F F *The uper board which is fastened to the other, wherein the rockets are placed.*

    G G *The wiers passing thorow both boards which are fastened to the foot of each anticke.*

    H H *The other wiers which stand fast in the fixed board, and are to turne about the antickes passing by them.*

CHAP. XXV.

Another way for making an anticke dance, which is not so violent as the former.

Ake one of your large sort of wheeles, and fasten it on an iron axeltree, so that the wheele move the axeltree with his motion; then let there bee a screw filed on the said axeltree, which may bee fitted to a small wheele of tenne teeth or thereabouts as you please, for the more teeth there is in the wheele, the slower it goeth, and easier, *et contra* : which wheele let it be so fastened to an axeltree, (on which the board bearing the antickes must stand) that the fire wheele turning about verticall, may move your worke hirozontall, which will move so slow, that the fire wheele will be tenne times about, before your Motion will move once about, which being done neatly, will prove a worke of great contentment. The forme whereof is expressed in the seventh Figure by the letter F.

A *The fire wheele placed on an iron axeltree, and made fast to it.*
B *The screw made on the said axeltree, or filed out of the same stuffe.*
C *The wheele which the aforesaid screw must be fitted to runne with, which must have so many teeth, as you intend the fire wheele shall move about for once of your motion.*
D *The square board on which the antickes stand, and is fastened to the axeltree which hath the wheele.*
E *A place for a light to burne so long as the worke indureth.*
F F F *The detentes or pieces which come thorow the board from the foot of each anticke.*
G G G *Certaine pinnes standing upright in the fixed board, to the end that the others passing by may be turned about.*

CHAP. XXVI.

How to compose a Castle of fire worke with the manner of placing the workes in a true order.

Repare a Castle of wood, or plate, of what large-nesse you please, the which shall bee made foure square, with round towers and battlements, and on the top or inner part of that worke, let there bee a lesser tower of the same fashion, with a Vane on the top, or such a like Figure, which having provided, let there be a place made close to the battlements, or within one inch of them, to lay your conveiances, (which let be of brasse) which is for your reports, which must be placed betweene each battlement, and shall have little pipes of brasse to give fire to each report, which must be screwed into the great conveiance;

ance; which conveiance let be filled with your composition for rockets of 1 l. which is one pound of powder to 3½ ℥ of coale dust; and by this meanes you shall have them all fire in order, without any confusion; which having spent it selfe, shall give fire to another conveiance, which shall be placed further in, with a strong wall betweene, so that the fire of one doe not offend the other: the use of this conveiance is to place divers rockets on, so that they may fire one after another, and shall take fire as soone as the reports are ended. Now for the foure large towers, you shal provide foure pieces of wood, turned and fitted to slide in exactly, and shall have divers smooth holes boared round thorow the out side of your tower, and the wood, till they meet with the hollow which passeth from the top to the bottome, or within an inch, which hollow shall bee one inch and a halfe diameter, and must be filled with a very slow mixture, (to the end it may continue as long as the worke is a burning) then place some Fisgigs round in those little holes, so that the mouths may be inward and primed, which will take fire one after another, and flye out on every side of your Castle, which will give great content : for the manner of firing this, I could wish, that it were first fired at the foure uper towers, and that through one of the corners, may bee a hole, which may goe to the uper conveyance, that so those reports may fire next, and at the end of that conveyance shall be another to passe downe to the lower tier of reports, and at each corner of that conveyance shall be a hole to passe into those lower towers, so that by that time all the reports are fired, the towers shall be all on fire; then at the end of that conveyance, (as I said before) let your conveyance for your rockets bee placed, which taking fire orderly, will conclude the worke. These and the like are for the pleasure of princes and great personages, rather then for the vulgar.   The forme of this Castle is said downe in the eight Figure by the letter A.

B B B *Expresseth the angles of the lower tower.*
C C C *The angles of the higher tower.*
D D *The conveiance that fires the reports.*
E   *The conveyance passing to the rockets.*
F F F *The Fisgigs placed round each angle.*
G G *Reports placed on the battlements.*
H H *Rockets placed farther in with a wall betweene.*

<hr />

Chap: XXVII.
How to represent divers motions in a Castle of fire-worke.

Ause a frame to be made, placing thereon two Castles, that they may stand about twelve foot distant one from another; this frame must bee so ordered, that it may bee hollow underneath, which being done, let the dores of those Castles bee placed the one opposite to the other, at each end of the said frame, and just within each doore, let there bee a

rowler

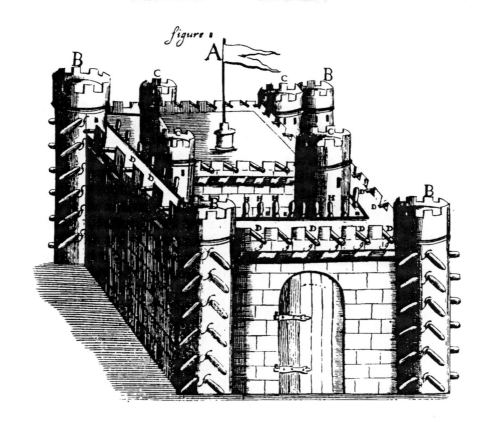

figure 1

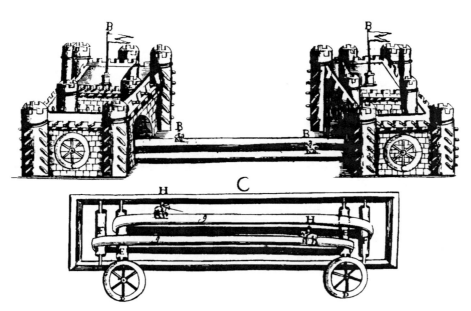

rowler of wood, foure inches diameter, which shall have iron pevikts or points to runne upon, that they may runne the more easie; and let those roulers be put full of small pinnes, and a girt put round about them, to the end that the rowlers moving circular, may draw the girt in a straight line, then placing some antike Figures on the girt (so that they may move about with it) place your fire wheeles upon the axeltree of each rowler, providing another rowler at each end to make it slide more easily; so firing the said wheeles, you shall see the antikes come one out of one doore, and the other at the other doore, meeting in the midst; and when they come at the contrary end, they make a returne with their heads downeward, and come up againe at the same doores they went first out of, which will continue running, so long as the fire wheeles continue. And when the wheeles stand still, the reports shall goe off on each tower one against another, which shall be done after this manner: let one of the spoakes of both your wheeles be hollow, and also part of the axeltree, which let be filled with powder dust, and the rocket which fires last, shall be placed over that spoake which hath the vent, with a piece of cotton wicke to fire it, so will it runne downe thorow the axeltree, which (as I said) must be hollow, and must have paper pasted over it, so that as soone as the fire comes there, it breakes thorow the paper, and fires a traine which is laid round about it, which traine passeth to a standing conveyance, which goeth up to the battlements, and so giveth fire to those reports; which having past each corner, the lower tower shall fire as it passeth, and from thence passe to an inner conueiance, which shall fire so many rockets, as may be well placed about it; this being well and orderly performed, will give great content. The forme whereof is expressed in the eight Figure, N B B.

B B *Represents the two Castles ready fitted with the frame.*
A A *The two doores opposite.*
B 　*The two figures moving forward.*
C C *The two fire wheeles which causeth this motion.*
C *Represents the frame for this motion.*
D D *The two fire wheeles fixed on their axeltree.*
E E *The Roler each wheele is fixed to.*
F F *The other Rolers which guide the girts.*
G G *The girts passing from one roller to the other.*
H H *The figures placed on the girts.*

CHAP.

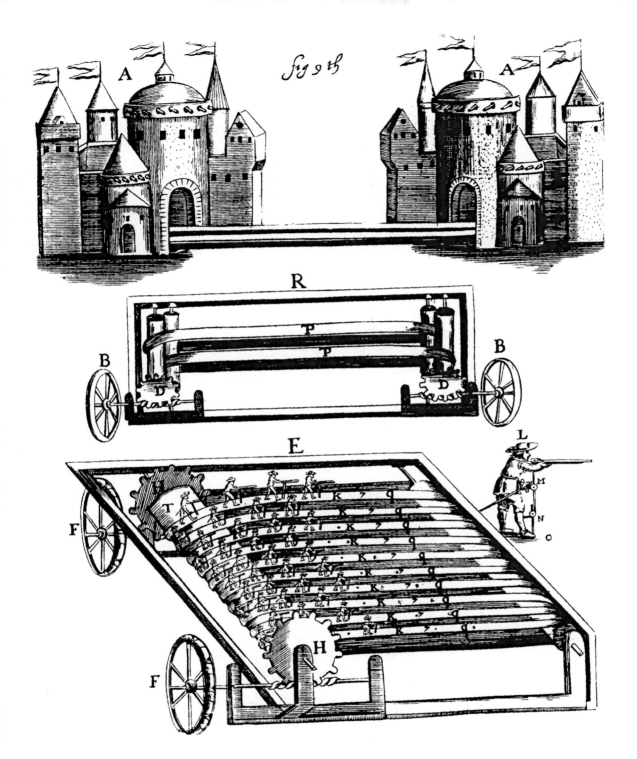

CHAP. XXVIII.

Another way to performe the same motions, and will not be so violent as the former.

Repare your Castle with the frame fitted as the former, onely upon the axeltree of each rowler, let there bee a small wheele with teeth, and likewise must there bee a screw upon the axeltree of each fire wheele; which must be so fitted, that they may draw these wheeles about, which if they be well fitted, will move them with great facilitie; and whereas the other fire wheeles were placed on each side, these must be placed behinde, or underneath, which you please, or finde most commodious. Now you must note that your fire wheele moving once about, moveth but one tooth of your other wheele by reason of the screw which drawes him, so that if you make tenne teeth in the said wheele, your fire wheele shall make tenne revolutions for one of your rowler: by this meanes it will move after a farre more easie manner then the former. The manner of this is represented in the ninth Figure, A A R.

A A *Represents the two Castles ready placed.*
R   *The frame for the motion.*
B B *Two fire wheeles which forceth the rest of the worke.*
C C *The screws fastened on the axeltree of each wheele, which forceth the rowlers.*
D D *The two wheeles which are placed on the rowlers, and fitted to the screw which force them.*
P P *The two girts on which the figures are placed.*

CHAP. XXIX.

How to represent the forme of an army of an hundred men marching, which shall present and fire at one certaine place appointed.

He ground of all these motions, are wheele workes; wherefore to proceed, you must provide a rowler of two foot long or more, which must be made and placed as the forementioned, to be drawne by two screwes fastened to the fire wheeles, in regard of the great weight they are to draw; also they must be somewhat large wheeles, with rockets of the second size, which is five ounces in each rocket, placing about each wheele, 20. or more, which having provided, you must like-

likewise get you so many figures of souldiers, which must bee cut by a Carver, and ought to have the joynts loose of the right arm of each, with a wyer or detent, to come down from the arm to the thigh of each, and likewise another, which may move that, and come to the foot ; then place these on severall girts, so that they may stand ten in ranck and file, and may be an inch between each, to the end they touch not at the feet, but every file may run in a severall groofe ; then placing small peeces in their hands, which must bee ready loaded and primed, set them going, and within two foot of the end of their march, let there bee a crooked peece of iron stuck up, between each file, so that they may stand inst in a straight line, to the end that when the souldiers move to that place, the detents or wyers are forced against those pins which draw back the arm, and so puls the trickers of each Peece in that ranck, so that the whole ranck will fire altogether, if they bee well ordered ; and as these have fired and past, another ranck moveth forward to the same place, performing the same ; thus continuing till they have all performed the like, which being finished, and all past, they shall make a second march, orderly without firing. This being well and carefully ordered, shall not faile, and will be a very rare work to behold, but will prove extraordinary costly to the owner thereof.

The form of this you shall finde in the ninth figure, by the letter R?

E *represents the whole frame, with all the parts thereof.*

F F *are the two fire wheeles, being placed one at each end of the rowler.*

G G *the screwes, being fastned to each fire wheele, which move the two wheeles placed on the rowler.*

H H *the two wheeles being placed at each end of the rowler.*

I I *two rowlers, about which the girts do passe, which carry the whole body of men.*

K K *the girts on which the figures are placed, each girt having upon it ten, so that in the whole there will be an hundred.*

L *represents the figure of a man standing in that posture as hee ought to bee made.*

M *Is the detent which is fastened to the right arme, and is to slide on a joynt, being fastened to the thigh ; so that it may move the arme.*

N *another detent which moveth the former, as it passeth by the pin.*

O *the pin which putteth by the said detent as it commeth to it.*

q q *the said pins in their right places.*

CHAP.

CHAP. XXX.

How to present musick playing, (by the help of fire) with anticks dancing.

Ause an instrument to bee made, representing the Virginals, and to it fit a Barrell set with severall tunes, (as I shall shew you in another Treatise hereafter) then let there be a wheele with teeth fastned on this barrell, and a fire wheele, with a screw on the axeltree, as I have shewed before, which screw may be so fitted, that as it moves round the barrell one way, so it may move another wheele, being placed on the side, which wheele shall move certain anticks, as the musick playeth. This and many more may bee performed by the motion of wheele work.

The form of this is expressed in the tenth figure, by the letter A.

B *the fire wheele, fixed on the axeltree, which moveth a screw.*

C *the screw, moving a wheele placed on the top of it, and another on the side.*

D *the wheele fastned to a barrell set with tunes.*

E *the wheele placed on the side, which hath a pinion at the end of the axeltree, marked F; which carrieth about the wheele G; on which there are placed foure anticks: this wheele moveth foure pinions marked H, on which is placed foure other anticks.*

I *is the barrell set with tunes.*

K *the pallats which causeth the jacks to move.*

L *the jacks which passe up to the strings.*

M *a board or frame covering the strings, on which is placed the anticks.*

Having spoken sufficiently of the order of motions performed by wheele work, I come now to shew some things that may bee done on the Line.

CHAP. XXXI.

How to make a Dragon, or any other creature to run on the Line, by the help of fire:

E T your Dragon be made either of pasteboard, or else of fine rods, such as your Basketmakers use; which must bee made hollow, with a place in the belly to put in two rockets, and shall bee so ordered, that there may come a small pipe from the tayle of one, to the head of the other; then make a place in the eyes, and mouth, to put into each hole fire, which shall be made up in rowled paper, and thrust in; then on the top of the back let there bee fastned two small pulleys for the line to run in, which being done, your Dragon is finished, to
firing,

firing, which muſt be thus ; firſt fire it at the eyes, and mouth, (alwayes noting, that this receipt muſt be ſome ſlow mixture, ſuch as your ſtarres) then fire that rocket which is placed with his mouth toward the tayle of the Dragon, which will make it ſeem to caſt fire from thence, till hee come to the end of his motion ; and then on a ſudden, as a creature wounded with ſome accident, ſhall return with fire coming forth of his belly, which being well ordered, will give great content.

The form of this you ſhall finde in the tenth figure, by the letter B.

B *repreſents a dragon to bee forced with rockets, which are placed in the belly.*

C *a place made to put in a rocket, which muſt be put in at the tayle, with the mouth of the rocket outward.*

D *is a conveyance from the tayle of that rocket, to the mouth of the next, which commeth out at the belly.*

E F *two ſmall braſſe pullees, faſtned in a frame on the back, for the line to run in.*

CHAP. XXXII.

Another way for making a fiery Dragon to paſſe on the line with-out the help of fire.

I N the former Chapter, I ſpake of a Dragon of a ſmall ſize, of a foot in length, or thereabout ; now I come to ſpeak of thoſe of a greater magnitude, which cannot ſo eaſily bee forced with fire, in a ſtraight line, without ſome artificiall help ; for Art muſt bee alwayes as a handmaid attending on Nature, to help her in her work ; therefore having prepared a large dragon, you muſt make divers hollow truncks of wood, within the body, which ſhall bee to caſt out fire, and on a ſudden divers ſmall bals of fire, other times a great number of ſmall fisgigs. Now to make this run on the line, you muſt have a hollow trunck faſtned on the back, between the wings of your dragon, which muſt bee ſomewhat bigger than your cord, with a ſmall hole thorow each end ; the uſe of thoſe ſmall holes is, to faſten a ſmall cord, which muſt be ſo faſtned, that one end thereof muſt bee faſtned at the head of the Dragon, and ſo paſſe over a pulley ; (which pulley ſhall bee faſtned at the end of the line) and returning thorow that hollow trunck in the back, it ſhall be put over another pulley at the other end of the line, and ſo making a return, ſhall be faſtned to the hole in the hinder part of the trunck. Now one of theſe pulleys ſhall have a handle or winch to turn it about, which ſhall cauſe the dragon to move, and ſhall be a help to the drawing of it backward and forward at your pleaſure ; after this manner you may form many works on the line, which other-wiſe cannot be done. The form of this is ſet down in the eleventh figure, by the letter A.

D

A

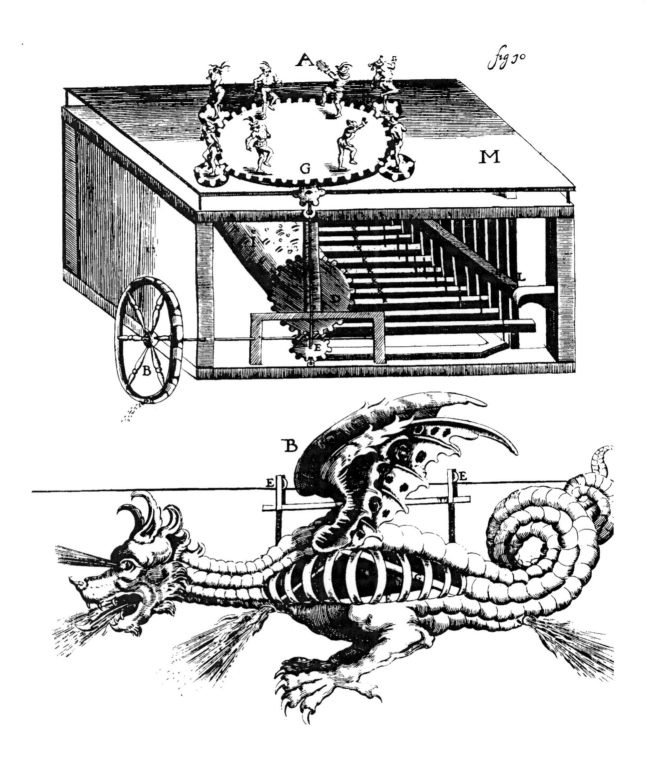

fig 10

A *representeth the dragon ready finished, with all his works.*

B C *the* *manner of the hollow trunck which the cord must passe thorow.*

B *the place for fastning of a small cord, which must passe over the pulley, marked* D.

D *the manner of fastning that pulley which must bee at the further end of the line.*

o o o o *the manner of the passing of the sayd line which is thorow the hollow trunck, and so over the pulley marked* E, *and then fastned to the other end of the trunck marked* G.

F *a handle or winch belonging to one of the pulleys which maketh the dragon move forward and backward, as occasion proscreth.*

H H *the great line on which the dragon passeth, and is only for keeping it steaddy in the motion.*

CHAP. XXXIII.

How to represent S. George *fighting with a Dragon in fire on the Line.*

Aving prepared your figures artificially made, you must make a hollow trunck thorow the body of each figure, for a great line to passe thorow, and likewise for a smaller line to draw them to and from each other ; which must bee fastned in this manner : at the breast of the dragon let one end of one cord be tied, which shall passe thorow the body of the George, and returning it about a pulley at the other end, fasten it to the back of the George, and at the breast of the George let another cord be tied, which shall passe thorow the body of the dragon, or a trunck on the back and so returning about a pulley at that end shall be pulled straight, and fastned to the tayle of the dragon, so that as you turn that wheele, the George and dragon will runne furiously at each other ; and when you please you may cause them to make a retreat, and come on againe divers times ; but in all these works forget not to sope your line extraordinary well, and likewise have a care that your work be not too heavy above the line, but that they may hang *equilibrio,* otherwise they will turn their heeles upward, which would bee a great disgrace to the work and workman : there might bee much written upon this same subiect, but to the ingenious, I think it is sufficient, they may order their works according to their own fancies ; only here is the ground of the matter. The manner of this is represented in the eleventh figure, by the letter B.

C *represening the George.*

D *the dragon.*

E *the small line fastned to the head of the dragon, and passeth thorow the body of the George.*

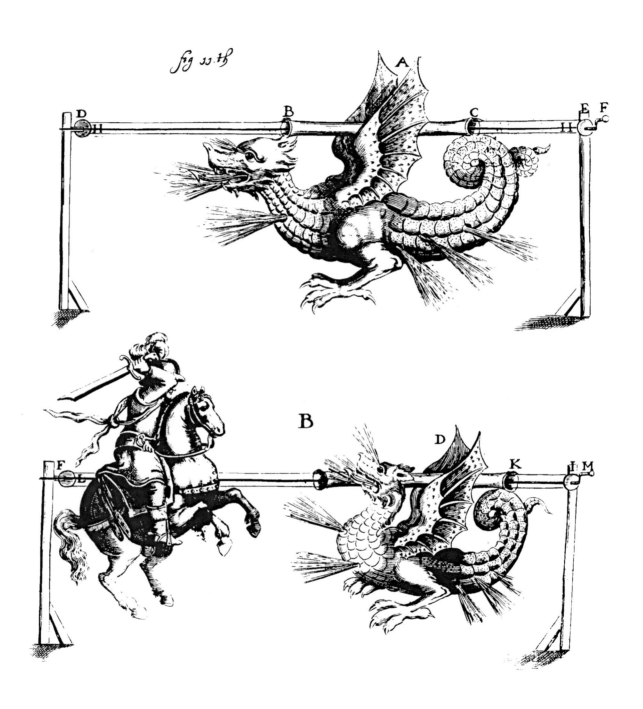

F *the pulley which guideth the said line.*

G *the place of fastning the other end of that line.*

H *another line fastned to the breast of the horse, which passeth thorow the hollow trunck of the dragon.*

I *the pulley about which it passeth, and is fastned to the tayle of the dragon.*

K *the place of fastning the said line to the dragon.*

L L *the great line which guideth these two figures.*

M *the winch or handle fastned to one of the pulleys, and is for the moving them forward or backward.*

CHAP. XXXIV.

How to make a trunck of fire, which shall cast forth divers fire bals.

Rovide a trunck of foure inch boare, and two foot long, with a hollow place in the bottom, of two inch boare, & as much deep, to the end it may be put on a strong post; let there be a bottom left between the two boares, which shall be two inches thick, so that there will be twenty inches left for your work, which shall bee filled as followeth; first fill it with corne powder one inch, then put in your ball, which shall bee five inches and a halfe, and round about it put powder dust, till you come to the top, then fill it two inches and a halfe with slow mixture, and on that two inches of corn powder : then put in another ball, and after it slow mixture, which shall be filled to the top, and so reserve it for your use ; note that you must turn three places for arming of it, which must be done either with iron hoops or else with cords, to the end the violence of your corn powder burst it not ; your upper ball shall be made after this manner : Having made ready a case of canvas, fill it with this mixture following.

Take
1 *l. of saltpeter.*
$\frac{1}{2}$ *l. of powder dust.*
$\frac{1}{4}$ *l. of sulphur vive.*
2 ℥ *of camphire.*
1 ℥ *of oyle of peter.*

Mix these very well, till it become somewhat tough, and then fill your ball, and arm it, leaving foure vents, into which you shall put foure small sticks, till such time you have coated; the manner of coating is, to dip the ball in a mixture of pich, rosin, tallow, and sulphur, but this is for bals of longer continuance ; the coating for this ball shall be as followeth ;

Take

The receipt for coating,
$\frac{1}{2}$ *l. of pitch.*
$\frac{1}{4}$ *l. of vernish.*
1 ℥ *of sulphur vive.*
2 ℥ *of powder dust.*

Melt your pitch and sulphur, and then poure in your vernish and pow-der dust, and while it is hot dip in your ball, and then cast a little fine powder dust over it, and so let it coole a little, and then dip it lightly a-gaine, and so you have it ready ; when you use it, pull out your foure sticks out of the vents, and fill them with powder dust, and so put them in. The lower ball which is last fired, shall be full of starres, with pow-der dust intermixed, to break the ball, these shall be primed with cotton wick made of purpose, to the end it may not fire the bal til it be up a good heighth, and then to break into a showre of starres.

The receipt of the composition for the trunck.
1 *l. of roch peter.*
$\frac{1}{4}$ *l. of fine powder dust.*
$\frac{1}{2}$ *of sulphur vive.*
2 ℥ *of camphir.*
1 ℥ *of linseed oyle.*

The forme of this trunck is represented in the twelfth figure by the letter A.

A *represents a trunck ready finished, with two bals.*
B *the ball which lieth uppermost, and is filled with slow composition.*
C *the lower ball, which is filled with starres,*
D *the slow mixture at the top of the trunck.*
E *the corn powder to send forth the upper ball.*
F *the second lay of composition.*
G *the powder for sending forth the lower ball.*
o o o *three places left for arming the said trunck.*
H *the bottom of the trunck, which must be two inches thick.*
I *a place left to put in a post of wood for it to stand on.*

CHAP. XXXV.

The manner of making a Club, which being fired, shall cast forth divers small works, or fisgigs.

Ause a peece of wood to be turned of foure inches diame-ter, boare it one inch and a halfe from the top toward the bottom, only leaving a bottom of an inch thick, and likewise a place underneath to put in your club staffe, the length of this trunck may be eighteen inches ; then draw a circular or spiral line, from the top to the bot-tom, which let bee in the manner of a screw, every thred being an inch and a halfe asunder, and in that line boare small holes, (of the bignesse of one of your fisgigs) till you come within a quarter of an inch of the bottom

tom of each hole ; and then pierce it with a small piercer, till you come to the soule of the trunck. Having done this, make small wyers fit to each hole, which let be fastned, so that they may stand opposite to the said holes, within two inches off from each hole ; the use of them is, to keep your fisgigs more upright and steaddy, which otherwise would bee apt to fall out, by reason they must bee put in very slack, or else they would not so easily come forth, when they should, then load your trunck with the slow mixture appointed in the former chapter (for a trunck) and put in your fisgigs, priming each, and likewise each hole, and so firing it at the top, you shall finde them come forth one after another, as your trunck burneth downwards, which shall scatter abroad after a confused manner. The form of this you shall see in the twelfth figure, by the letters EI.

E represents the form of the club without the wyers on, or any other work.
I is the said club ready finished with all his work.
K the wyers placed for to stay each fisgig in his place.
L the fisgigs placed.
M the place of firing.
N the club fast put into the bottom.

Chap. XXXVI.

Another sort of club, which being fired, shall give many reports.

Rovide a club like unto the former, but let not the holes be boared so big, but only that a small quill or pipe may go in for a vent to every breaker, then having boared your holes at proportionable distance, cut so many hollow groofes with a googe or halfe round chisell, and fit them to your breakers of paper, and place so many reports round about it ; your reports or breakers for this work shall bee made as followeth ; upon a rowler of halfe an inch, rowle so much paper till you make it an inch thick, and better, choaking it close at one end, then fill it an inch and a halfe with good pistoll powder, choaking it at the other end, so that it be very close at each end ; then pierce a small hole in the middle for a pipe to enter in, which must bee filled with powder dust, and put into the small holes of your trunck, very close, then pitch them well round about, and poure pitch all over, that the work may not be seen ; and likewise that it may hold your reports close together ; this pitch likewise when the fire commeth to it, will easily fire, and make a very furious light, which will give great content. The form of this is represented in the twelfth figure by the letters O and V.

O representing the club without the reports placed.
A the groofes to put in the reports, with a hole in the middle of each groofe to put in the quill.
R a report with a quill ready to be placed in the club.

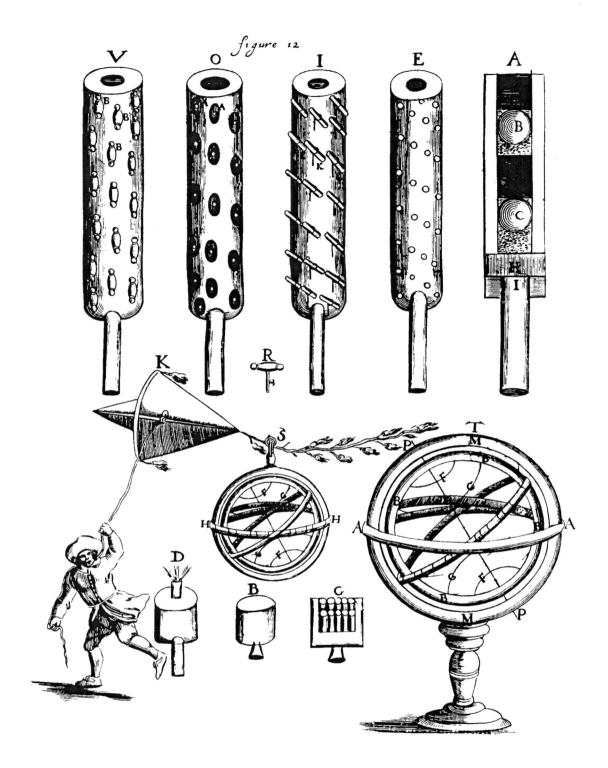

figure 12

q *the manner of the quill which muſt bee put into thoſe ſmall holes to fire the reports.*

V *the club finiſhed, with the reports placed in it.*

B B *the manner of the reports as they are placed in the ſaid club.*

CHAP. XXXVII.

Another, which I call Iack in a box.

THE order of making this is after this manner; provide a box of plate, of what largeneſſe you pleaſe, which let be ſix inches deep, with a ſocket at the bottom to put in your ſtaffe, then putting in a quantity of corn powder or powder duſt, (in the bottom of the box) you ſhall fill it with fiſgigs, or ſerpents, leaving a place in the middle for a cane to go thorow to the bottom, which cane muſt be filled with ſlow receipt, in which you ſhall put a quantity of camphir, but no oyles, in regard of the narrow paſſage it hath to burn, without any other vent; then put your cane down, leaving it an inch above the box, and take a peece of thick paſtebord, cutting a hole for the cane to paſſe thorow, and glew it cloſe to the cane, to the end the fire paſſe not thorow before the appointed time; this paſtebord muſt bee of ſufficient breadth to cover your box quite over, then put it on a ſtaffe, and light your cane, which will appeare only like a candle, and after a pretty diſtance of time you ſhall heare a ſudden noyſe, and ſee all thoſe fiſgigs flying ſome one way, ſome another. This toy hath given great content to the ſpectators. The form of this is ſet down in the twelfth figure by the letters B C D.

B *the box without any thing in it.*

C *the fiſgigs placed in the box.*

D *the box finiſhed, with a cane paſſing thorow to the bottom.*

CHAP. XXXVIII.

How to repreſent the Sphere, moving in the ayre, without any other ſupportation.

Auſe a Sphere to bee made ſomewhat light, and on the horizon place your rockets, and in the zenith or upper part, let there bee a pinne paſſe thorow the meridian, with a ring faſtned to it, to hang it by; this muſt bee faſtned to a large Kite, ſo as the Sphere may hang ſix foot under it, then faſten a match of cotton to the noſe of the firſt rocket, and light it, which having done, raiſe your Kite, and

by

by such time as it is at the highest, the rockets shall take fire, and shall cause it to make divers revolutions in the ayre; you may place the midst of this sphere full of lights, which will seeme very strange. The manner of this is represented in the twelfth Figure, by the letters K and S.

K *Represents the Kite which is supported by the ayre, and to which the sphere is fastened.*
S *The sphere with all his circles, the rockets being placed about the horizon.*
H H *The horizontall circle about which the rockets are placed.*

Chap. XXXIX.

How to represent the sphere, with divers circles, some moveable, others fixed.

Ause a spheare to be made, either of wood or mettall, the outward circles representing the meridian circle with the horizon, the next within shall represent the Collurs with the equinoctiall, likewise the tropicks and zodiacke, whose poles shall be 23 degrees ½ from the poles of the world; by which meanes the eclipticke shall bee excentricke to the equinoctiall, (which shall be expressed) so that fastening rockets about the equinoctials, and placing two small lights in the zodiacke, the one representing the Sunne, the other the Moone: you shall see them move about the earth, (which is placed in the midst of the spheres) according to the rules of *Ticho Brahe,* and shall be according to their naturall manner of motion, which is continually rising and setling in an oblique motion to the horizon and meridian, which alwaies stand fixed, and the rest moving on the poles of the equinoctiall, although the eclipticke bee framed from its owne poales. The forme of this is represented in the twelfth Figure, by the letter T.

M *The fixed Meridian.*
A A *The Horizon.*
E E *The Equinoctiall.*
E E *The Eclipticke with the Sunne and Moone placed round.*
P P *The poles or axeltree about which all the inner circles move.*

CHAP. XL.

How to make a halfe moone of Rockets to appeare in the ayre.

Rovide a piece of planke of two inch thicke, and turne it to a halfe round, then cut so many groves (from the center to the circumference) as you intend to place rockets about it, and on the other side, let there be rings for every rod to passe thorow, of which let one of each bee close to the top, and another neere the end of each rod; and note that the planke must be so large, that the ends of all the rods must meet in the center; then prime each rocket with a quill filled with powder dust, and put on the top of each groofe, till you have placed your semicircle full; then having primed these groofes, (which comes from one center to the circumference) paste paper over them, and so let it stand till you fire it, which is done after this manner: set this same at the top of a poast, about foure or five foot from the ground, and prime it (at the center) with a little cotton wicke prepared for that purpose, and firing it, you shall see them take fire all at one instant, and so will flye circular, in the forme of a halfe Moone. The forme whereof is represented in the thirteenth Figure, by the letters A B.

A *Represents the forepart of the frame, in which one presents the groofes which passe to each rocket.*

D D *The quils filled with powder dust, entring into the groofes with one end, and into the rocket with the other.*

B *Represents the backe part of the frame.*

E E *The rings below.*

F F *The rings above.*

G G *The rockets placed on the frame.*

CHAP. XLI.

How to make a case of Rockets to rise at once.

Ause a frame to bee made about two foot square, with small groofes, two inches asunder, and betweene each groofe, boare holes for your rocket rods to passe thorow; you may make tenne groofes, and in each groofe you may place ten rockets, so you shall haue a hundred rockets in one of these cases, which shall fire all at once; there must bee a crosse groofe made in the middest, and in the center of that groofe, shall you fire it, which shall suddenly fire all over, being primed with a quicke traine of powder: the charge is great, and quickly spent, but it makes a very glorious shew.

The forme of this is represented in the **13** Figure, by the letters G D.

AAAA

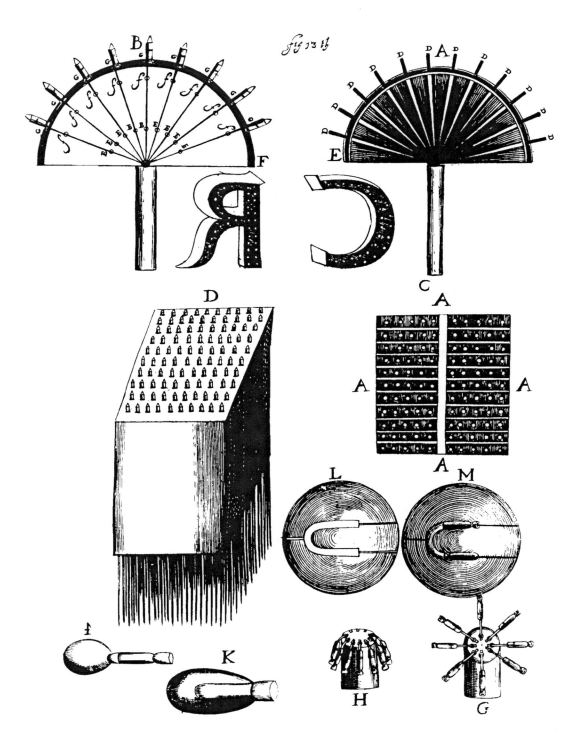

fig 13 th

A A A A *Reprefents the fquare of your cafe which is grooved.*

The white ftraakes fignifie the groofes which are to be filled with powder duft, whereon the mouth of your rockets muft be placed.

The other fpaces expreffe the holes where your rods paffe thorow with a hole in the midft to fire it at.

B *Reprefents the cafe filled with rockets, their rods paffing thorow, and is made long, to the end there may be another board at the bottome for each rod to paffe thorow, that they may be kept more fteady.*

CHAP. XLII.

How to make letters or any other figure appeare in the ayre, after the fpending of a Rocket.

Aving confidered of what largeneffe you will have your letters or figures, make them of paftboard, leaving a hollow to put in fmall quils, (which fhall bee filled with a cleare and ftrong mixture) then put in your quils, and glue them faft in; and and fo have you finifhed it, till you come to ufe it. There is another manner, which is thus; provide a mould of plate, and cut out what letter you pleafe in waxe, which having done, fticke it full of quils in an orderly forme, and put this on the head of your rocket: note this, that thefe are onely to be ufed on very large rockets. The forme of thefe are reprefented in the thirteenth Figure E F.

The forme of the letters, the white fpots fignifying the place for fo many quills filled full of flow mixture, to be placed in.

CHAP. XLIII.

How to reprefent a figure of the Sunne cafting forth his beames, in fire.

Aufe a boxe to be made of plate, too inches long, and one inch diameter, which muft be filled with your flow compofition, and let the head be made with fmall groofes, croffing the center, to the end you may lay in certaine fprings of fteele, fuch as they ufe to fmall Watches. Thefe fprings fhall bee about fixe inches in length, and muft be foure, fo that both ends of each appearing, will make eight, which will make a circular forme, the boxe being the center; now to the end of every one of thefe fprings, muft be faftened one of your fmall Fifgigs, & then bent up clofe to the boxe, and fo put into your coffine at the

E top

top of your rocket, with powder duſt and cotton to fire and breake the
coffine, which as ſoone as it breakes, the ſprings will caſt forth your Fiſgigs, and make them ſeeme like the ſparkling beames of the ſunne, and
the mixture in the center will ſeeme as the body of the ſame; this will
continue a while, and then you ſhall ſee it breake with divers reports.
This I had from a noble Captaine of this City, namely Captaine *Fore-*
ſtar, who invented the ſame, the forme whereof is repreſented in the
thirteenth Figure, by the letters L M.

    L *Being the boxe with the ſprings faſtened to the top, with a Fiſgig at the*
end of each.
    M *The ſaid boxe finiſhed with the ſprings bent ready to put on the head of a*
Rocket; the mouth of each Fiſgig muſt come downe to the mouth of the boxe,
and ſo be put with their mouthes all downewards.

Having ſpoken ſufficiently of workes operating in the ayre, I will ſhew
you ſomething which ſhall ſerve for ground workes.

CHAP. XLIV.

How to make a Rocket which firing it out of your hand, ſhall con-
tinually be in agitation on the ground ſometimes, and
other whiles about in the ayre.

Aving prepared a Rocket, with a report in the head, tye it
to a bladder, ſo that the end of the Rocket may come to
the mouth of the bladder, and binde it over very ſtrong-
ly, then firing it out of your hand, caſt it away from
you, it matters not which way, for it will come to the
ground, and by reaſon of the bladder, it cannot ſtay, but
preſently rebounds upward, moving to and fro, till it be all ſpent. There
is another ſort, and that is a ſmall Rocket put into a bladder, and ſo
blowne up round about it, and tyed about the necke of the Rocket. The
forme of theſe are repreſented in the 13 Figure, by the letters G H.

    G *The Rocket with the bladder at the taile of it.*
    H *The Rocket in the bladder.*

CHAP.

CHAP: XLV.

How to make a ball which shall be in continuall agitation on the ground, till the fire is consumed.

Ause a ball to be made of some light wood, which must be made so, as you may take it asunder just in the midst, then make on each side a hollow groofe to lay in two rockets (joyned together after the manner of your runners) so close up your ball fast with glue; onely in the place where the two Rockets joyne, shall be a groofe, which shall be pasted over with paper, that the second rocket firing, may have a vent, otherwise your ball will serve but once. Then fire it, and you shall have your desire. This is represented in the 13 Figure by the letters I K.

I *Represents a part of the ball, as it is ready to place in the Rockets.*
K *Represents the ball, with the Rockets placed in, so that the other side being joyned, makes a perfect round.*
C C C *The vents to each Rocket, which being closed, must have paper glued over them, that they be not seene.*

CHAP. XLVI.

How to make another sort of Balles for the ground, which will be a long time in their motion.

Ause a ball to be made of some light wood, and let it bee hollowed, to make it the lighter; then fit in two pieces of wood, so that you may make both sides equall, which pieces of wood shall be so groofed, that you may lay in so many Rockets as may well be contained about it, providing that at the end of each groofe or rocket, you may have a vent thorow your ball, then place in your rockets as I have shewed you for the wheele: which having done, glue them fast in, to the end, that by the motion of the ball, they may not be disordered, then ioyne your ball together, and glue it fast with paper round about it, to the end the vents may be covered, onely leaving one open to fire it, so have you this ball finished, which firing, will continue a long while in motion, Figure 36.

A *The ball turned hollow with groofes to lay in your rockets.*
B *The other part of the ball, with the rockets fastened in.*
C C C C *The vents at the end of each rocket.*

CHAP. XLVII.

How to make a Dragon iffuing forth of a Cave, which fhall caft out much fire.

Rovide a Dragon of fome light matter, as wicker rods or the like, which let bee made fo, that you may put into the midft of the body, one of your greateft rockets, and clofe under the belly let there be a couple of wheeles, which fhall bee fo placed in the belly of the Dragon, that no part may bee feene, but onely the bottome which comes to the ground; and let the rocket bee fo placed, that it may with traines fire all parts of the body, as the eyes, mouth, and all other parts; in which you fhall place divers fmall workes, which firing, fhall flye out, and make a very great fhew, which fhall burne till all bee confumed: this Dragon muft be fo placed, that he may come forth of a feeming cave; which firing on a fudden, will make a great noyfe. by reafon of the largeneffe of the rocket, and the hollowneffe of the cave hee comes forth of. The forme whereof is reprefented in the fourteenth Figure by the letter G.

G *The Dragon ready finifhed.*
A *The wheeles on which it muft runne, which muft bee hid within the body.*
B *The rocket placed in the body of the Dragon, which caufeth the motion.*
G *The vent which paffeth to this rocket for the firing.*

CHAP. XLVIII.

How to make two Dragons to meete each other, from feverall Caves, which fhall fend forth their fire to each other with great violence.

Aving prepared two Dragons (both of one fize and weight) after the manner as I have fhewed you in the former Chapter; it is requifite that you know how farre they will runne, then place the Caves at fuch a diftance one from the other, that they may meete each other in the mid way, and that you may doe this the more neater, you fhall have your ground laid with fmooth boards that they may runne more free, and from the midft of the walke, to the end of each Dragon; let there be a groofe made in one of the boards, which fhall ferve to convey a traine to each, for the firing of them; then you fhall be fure, that if you fire it in the midft, they will both take fire together; alwaies provided you make a conveyance of paper from the board to the taile of each Dragon, or to the mouth of each rocket, which being fired once, they shall meete, and caſt forth their fire at each other with great violence. The forme of this is repreſented in the fourteenth Figure, by the letters A A.

A A *The two Dragons ready to runne.*
B B *The two great rockets which forceth them.*
C C *The wheeles which each Dragon runneth on.*
D *The midſt of their walke, with the groofe to each rocket.*

There are divers other workes which may bee performed after this manner, which for brevity ſake I will omit.

Likewiſe there are divers motions to bee performed by the action of man, as ſingle duels, to which appertaine the Buckler of fire, and likewiſe the Curtlax or Fauchion, the manner of which hath beene formerly deſcribed by divers Authors, almoſt in all languages, and therefore will ſeeme more then requiſite to relate thoſe things ſo large as they might be; for what action cannot man performe by his induſtry? and therefore I leave every man to his owne order, onely I will ſhew you the making of one ſort of Bucklar, which as yet hath not beene performed, and likewiſe the Fauchion or Curtlax, and firſt for the Bucklar.

Chap: XLIX.

How to make a Bucklar which ſhall caſt forth a hundred Fiſgigs, every one making his report.

Auſe a Bucklar to bee made of ſome light wood, which let be about two foot in diameter or more, as you pleaſe, then cauſe a groofe to bee cut in it, from the center to the circumference in a ſpirall or ſerpentine forme, then fill that groofe with one of your ſlow compoſitions, ſuch as hath neither oyle nor gummes, by reaſon the fume thereof may not offend the Bearers; when you have filled it, fit in pieces of wood, which may have holes to receive a quantity of Fiſgigs let every one bee two inches aſunder, and let there be wyer rings to every one of your Fiſgigs to hold them ſteady, that they fall not out, till ſuch time they fire, then put in your Fiſgigs, into every hole one, till you come to the center, and then ſhall you have a very great breaker, ſo that firing it at the circumference, every Fiſgig will flye out as the fire comes to it, and will flye againſt his adverſary combatant, till they come both to the center, and then will they give a great report, and ſo end. The forme of this is repreſented in the 14 Figure by the letters F G.

F *Repreſents the Buckler as it muſt be grooved.*
G *Repreſents the ſame finiſhed, with the Fiſgigs placed about it.*
H H *Repreſents the manner of uſing the ſaid Buckler, with the Fauchion.*

fig 14

CHAP. L.

How to make the Curtlax, Cimiter, or Fauchion.

PRepare a Curtlax either of wood, or plate, which let bee hollowed from back to edge, three inches, and let it bee so thick, as it may serve for your smallest fisgigs, then you shall have a peece of pastebord so fitted on the back, that your work may be close covered, only holes left for the ends of your fisgigs to come forth ; then you shall lay in your lances of fire (which is nothing else but your slow composition for starres put into hollow truncks of paper made on an arrow) and between every lance you shall put two or three fisgigs, which shall fly out so soon as the fire commeth to them ; having done this, you have finished your Fauchion, which must bee fired at the point, and so burn downward towards the hilt. This hath been formerly set forth by Monsieur *Thybaviel* a French Author, and since by divers others. The forme whereof is represented in the fourteenth figure, by the letters I K L.

I *represents the Fauchion prepared, with a groofe in the back.*
K *represents the Fauchion, with holes to put in the works.*
L *represents a Fauchion wholly finished, with the fisgigs placed as they ought to stand.*

Having spoken sufficiently of land works, I will come in the next place to shew the making of some works to bee acted on the water ; and first of all I will shew you the making of the water bals.

CHAP. LI.

How to make a water ball, which shall burn on the water, with great violence.

FIrst, having considered of what bignesse you will have your ball, take the circumference and halfe it, and of that halfe make a circle, which cutting out in strong canvas, shall bee halfe a case, so that sewing two of them together, they shall make a case according to your desire ; *For Example* ; I have a ball to make whose diameter is six inches, then the circumference (being as seven to twenty two) must be $18\frac{6}{7}$, so the halfe will bee $9\frac{3}{7}$, which must bee the diameter of your cloth, and must bee made true round, so that sewing two together, and making a case thereof, it shall bee almost six inches, which the arming will make good ; having made your case, you shall proceed to the filling of it, which shall be done after this manner ; you shall first put in three or foure good
spoonfuls

spoonfuls of your mixture, and then with a stick (made round at one end) force it close together, and so continue filling it, and between every filling put in your stick, and force it together, rounding it continually in your hand, till such time you have finished it ; which having done, sew it up close, and then arm it with small cord, which is called marling ; after you have done that, you shall coat it with a quantity of rosin, pitch, and tallow dissolved, and so your ball dipped over in the same, providing alwayes that you leave two vents to fire it, which shall be pierced a third part into your ball, and must bee stopped with small sticks, till such time you come to use them, then pulling forth the sticks, fill the two vents with fine powder dust, and firing it, cast it into the water, and you shall have your desire ; you must alwayes let your ball be thorow fired before you cast it from you.

A receipt for this ball.

Take 1 *l.* of *powder.*
        8 ℥ of *rochpeter.*
        4 ℥ of *sulphur.*
        2 ℥ of *camphir.*
        1 ℥ of *oyle of peter.*
        1 ℥ of *oyl of linne.*
        ⅓ ℥ of *oyle of spike.*
        2 ℥ of *colophania,*

The forme of this ball is represented in the fifteenth figure by the letters A B.

A A *the canvas ready cut, to be sewed together.*
B *the ball finished.*
C C *the two vents.*
D *a peece of cord left to hold it by whilst you coat it, and likewise to hang it up being finished.*

CHAP. LII.

A water ball which shall shoot forth many reports.

Ause a ball to be made of wood, which shall bee in two peeces, so that you may joyne it close together at pleasure ; this ball must have small holes boared round about it, to put in your quils, which must fire your reports ; the reports or breakers shall bee made of paper choaked at both ends, and primed thorow the midst ; they shall bee fastned round with pitch, and so covered round about, that no water may passe in ; you shal fil this bal in two halfes, to the end you may force it very close together, and when it is filled, giew it fast, and arm it well with nealed wyer, then put in your breakers, with a quill
                                                                which

which fhal enter into the bal, and likewife into the breaker ; the forme whereof you fhall fee in the fifteenth figure, by the letter C. The receipt for this bal muft be fomewhat flower than the laft, by reafon of the many vents it wil have, as the reports paffe away.

The receipt for this ball.

Take 1 *l.* of rochpeter.
4 ℥ of powder duft.
3 ℥ of fulphur vive.
2 ℥ of camphir.
1 ℥ of linfeed oyle.
2 ℥ of rofen.
1 ℥ of oyle benedick.

Powder that which is to bee powdered, and incorporate them well together, and by little and little fprinckle your oyles, til you have wrought it like a pafte, and then make ufe of it ; your quils which you prime with fhal be filled only with powder duft, to the end it fire fuddenly before the quil come to fhrink up, which wil be with a flow mixture.

A *the mouth of the ball where it is to be fired.*
B B B *the reports or breakers, being made of paper, and filled with corne powder.*
C C C *the quils, which are primed with powder duft, and ferve for firing the reports.*
D *the hollow of the ball, being filled with the flow compofition.*

CHAP. LIII.

How to make a Water ball, which, after a certaine time of firing, fhall caft forth divers rockets into the ayre.

Repare a ball of wood, of eight inches diameter, and boare a hole in the midft (of an inch and a halfe) and let it come within one inch of the bottom, and round about that great hole you fhall boare eight fmaller holes of an inch, fo that they may bee fit for eight rockets ; thefe holes fhall be an inch from the greater, and fhall all meet in one at the bottom ; wherefore you fhall cut off the bottom of the ball, and fit another to it, which may be fo hollowed, that your mixture may be conveyed to all the rockets, then faften on the bottom (having filled it with your mixture) and put in your rockets, with the mouth of each rocket downward, pafting paper round about it, which fhall bee coated with rofin and tallow, and over each hole where the rockets are placed, let it be foaped over the tallow, to the end that being fired, the fparks may not eafily take fire of the paper, which otherwife would make fome confufion ; having done this, fit in a peece of wood to the greater boare of your ball, leaving only a fmaller vent, of halfe an inch, and by this

meanes

meanes the fire will come out with more violence, and having spent it selfe, within one inch of the bottom, it shall fire the eight rockets placed about, which by their force shall break the paper of each, and ascend into the ayre, a small heighth, and after lie tumbling on the water. This ball is represented in the twelfth figure by the letter D.

A *the place of firing the ball.*
B B *the peece of wood put in to lessen the vent.*
C *the greater hollow to be filled with the slow composition as the former.*
D D *the bottom, which is loose, and to bee hollowed to receive part of the slow mixture.*
E E *the holes boared to put in the rockets, which must bee covered with paper.*
F F *the rockets placed in, with their mouthes downward.*
G G *the place of fitting the rockets.*

CHAP. LIV.

Another sort of water ball, which shall cast forth rockets at two sundry times, and after it is finished, shall give a great report.

His ball shall be made after the manner of the other, but shall bee a foot in diameter, and shall have two circles of rockets placed round about, so that the lower circle shall be one inch from the higher, and likewise shall go down into the ball an inch lower, and under that row of rockets there shall be placed a breaker of iron, which shall bee one inch from the lower tyer, so that the ball being fired, shall after a certain time, cast forth a dozen of small rockets, and then continue a while longer, and then in regard of the larger circumference of that circle, it shall cast forth twenty, and after that is ended, their fire comming to the chamber of iron, shall cause a very great report, and so conclude. The form of this is layd down in the fifteenth figure by the letter H.

H *the vent for firing the ball.*
I I *the peece of wood fitted to the greater boare.*
K *the hollow of the greater boare filled with a slow composition.*
L L *the upper tyer of rockets.*
M M *the lower tyer of rockets.*
N *the breaker of iron.*
o o o o *the places to put in the rockets, which must bee covered with paper well soaped, upon tallow.*

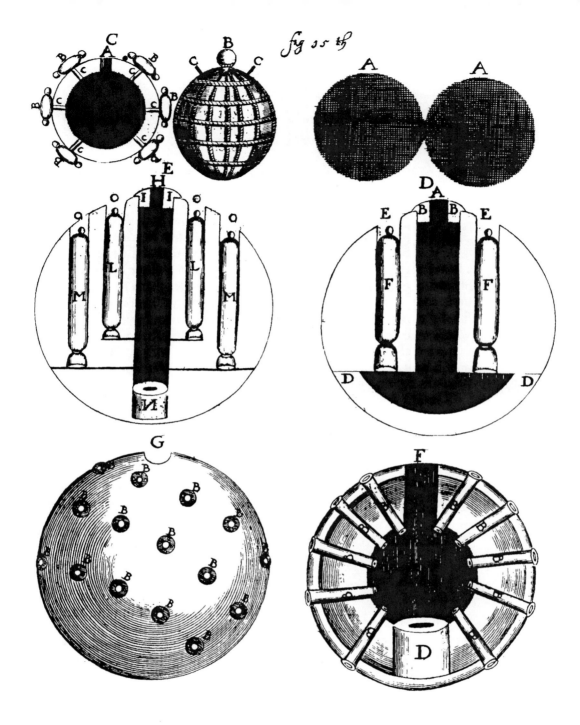

fig 35th

CHAP. LV.

*Another fort of ball, with iron chambers, every one casting
forth a small ball.*

Aufe a ball to be made, of twelve inches diameter, and in
the midst boare a large hole of two inches high, hollow-
ing it within, and let it come within an inch of the bottom; then boare small holes of an inch from the top to
the bottom, in a spiral line, to put in your smal chambers, which shall be made of iron, each chamber having
a broad plate at the mouth to fasten it to the ball ; those chambers shal
be loaden with a quantity of corn powder, and after that a smal ball made
up in canvas, and primed, as I have shewed you for starres, then having
filled the large concave with slow composition, place in your chambers,
whose touch holes or vents must bee just at the breech, and shal come al
in toward the center of the ball, then coat it round with rosin and tallow,
and so have you this bal finished ; the form whereof is represented in the
fifteenth figure, by the letter A.

The first figure marked F, represents the inside of the bal.

F the mouth of it.
B B the iron chambers, as they lie with the touch hole or vent of each chamber, at the breech of the same.
C the concave filled with slow composition.
D a large chamber placed at the bottom: note, that this ball must bee made
in two peeces, to place in this chamber, and after glewed well, and bound about
with wyer.

The second figure marked G, is the bal finished, except the coating.

G the vent at the mouth.
B B the reports, with a plate of iron round the mouth of each, to nayle it
fast.

This bal being thus provided, must be after covered with canvas, and
then dipped in a mixture of three parts rosin, two parts pitch, and one
part tallow, which must bee first incorporated on the fire, and so used :
this bal may serve as wel for service in warre, as for pleasure or triumph,
by putting into each chamber a bullet of lead, and so shot out of a Morter peece.

CHAP

CHAP. LVI.

There are divers other sorts of bals, as well for water as for land, and are to be shot out of the Morter peece.

ND becauſe the Morter peece is often uſed in Fire-works, I will deſcribe the manner of it, with the uſe thereof, as much as is requiſite to this place: and firſt for the manner; the manner of the Morter peece conſiſteth only in his proportions, which are divers, according to the pleaſure of the work-man; but thoſe of moſt uſe for fire bals, are one and a halfe, and two diameters, in the length of the chaſe, and one diameter in the length of the chamber, with halfe a diameter at the mouth of the chamber; the reaſon of this ſhortneſſe is, that one may come the more commodiouſly to the firing of the ball; the proportion of this peece followeth in the ſixteenth Figure.

B *is the form of a Morter peece lying on his carriage, the quoyn being made to draw with a ſcrew, as I have made uſe of.*

A A *the diameter or heighth of the boare, which is* 4¼ *inches, or* 100 *parts of this ſcale.*

A B *the length of the chaſe, and is two diameters, or* 8½ *inches.*

B B *the heighth of the chamber, which is halfe a diameter of the ſhot, which is here two inches.*

B C *the length of the chamber, which is one diameter of the ſhot, that is foure inches.*

C C *the bottom of the chamber, which is one inch, or* ¼ *diameter.*

D D *the diameter of the trunions, which is halfe the diameter of the ſhot, and is two inches.*

D E *the length of the trunions, and is two inches.*

The proportion of powder for this peece is 2⅝ for a ſtone ſhot, and 1⅝ for a Fire ball.

CHAP. LVII.

How to make a ball for the Morter peece, which ſhall caſt forth a great ſhowre of ſtars at the breaking.

His ball muſt bee made of canvas, and muſt bee ſo propor-tioned, that being armed (as I have formerly ſhewed) it may iuſt fit the chaſe of your peece, which being rea-dy, you ſhall proceed to the filling of it, which muſt be after this manner; at the bottom of this ball put in an ounce of fine corn powder, and then put in ſome of your round ſtarres well primed, and ſo fill them up cloſe about with powder duſt, ſtill putting in more of thoſe ſtarres, and in the midſt put

Γ one

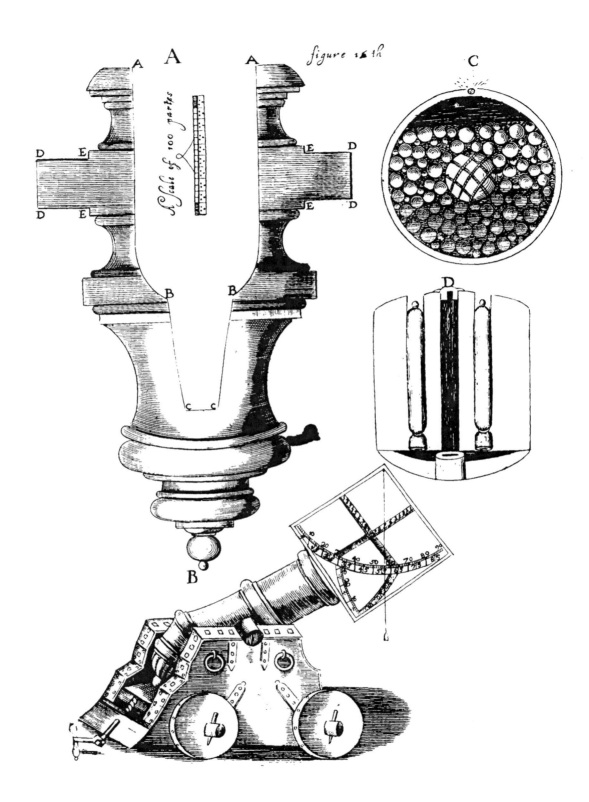

figure 16th

A Scale of 100 partes

one ſtarre which may be ſomewhat great, ſo filling it till you come within one inch of the top, then fill it up with a ſlow receipt, as I have formerly preſcribed for bals; and ſew it cloſe up, arming it with fine cord, or marline; and pierce a vent in that place where your ſlow mixture lyeth, alwaies provided you pierce it not too deepe, that your ball breake not before his appointed time: then when you would uſe it, loade your morter piece with one ounce of corne powder, putting after a wadd and tampion, and put on your ball with the vent towards the mouth of your piece: ſo elevating your piece toward the Zenith, you may proceed to the firing of it, which muſt be after this manner : provide two matches ready lighted, having one in each hand, and firſt fire your ball with one hand, and preſently give fire to your Piece with the other, alwaies holding your head under the horizontall line of your Piece, for feare the blaſt annoy you: this having done, you ſhall ſee your ball mount very high, with a faire taile of fire, and when it is at higheſt, ſhall breake forth into a goodly ſhowre of ſtarres : one of theſe bals will containe almoſt one hundred ſmall ſtarres. The forme of it is repreſented in the 16 Fiigure, by the letter G.

C Repreſenting the ball cut in ſunder, that you may ſee the order of the ſtars lying.

E The great ſtarre in the midſt, with all the reſt placed about it. Note every one of theſe ſtars muſt be primed thorow with cotton wicke, as I have formerly ſhewed.

D The ſlow mixture, which commeth within one inch of the top.

CHAP. LVIII.

Another ſort of ball for the morter piece, which ſhall caſt forth divers Rockets in the ayre.

His ball muſt be made of wood, according as I have formerly ſhewed you, onely it muſt be made proportionable to the piece, and moreover the vent which in the other is required to be a ſlow mixture, in this muſt bee more ſwift, in regard it would otherwiſe continue till it came to the ground, wherefore the mixture that this ball ſhall be filled with, ſhall be the ſame that your rockets of one pound are, which is 4 ⅝ of coleduſt to a pound of powder, and one ounce of ſaltpeter. Theſe muſt be well mealed, and likewiſe muſt be cloſe driven, otherwiſe it will conſume too faſt. This ball may bee made ſomewhat cillindricall, in regard of the length of the rockets to be placed in it, as you have made this for to caſt forth once, ſo you may make another to caſt forth twiſe, as I have formerly ſhewed you for the water ball. The forme is repreſented in the 16 Figure, by the letter D.

Chap. LIX.

How to compose a ship of fire workes, which being once fired, divers motions shall present themselves.

Ause a mould to be made so, as you may take off the upper decke, to place some workes underneath, where you shall have a fire wheele placed with a screw on the axeltree; this wheele shall bee placed in the sterne, and shall turne a rowler, on which shall be two girts placed, which shall passe on each side of the maine mast, and runne on to the foreship; in this wheele there shall be a hollow spoake and axeltree, as I have formerly shewed, which shall be so ordered, that the wheele being spent, it may convey fire to a tier of gunnes lying round about, which shall be fired with a close conveyance, and having passed that, it shall take hold of another conveyance, which shall give fire to certaine rockets, being placed in the bodies of some figures representing Mariners, and shall be so fitted, that they may have a cane joyned to the body to guide them, so that they may runne up from the top of the deck, to the top of each mast: this and many the like may bee performed with great facility. The forme of this is represented in the 1 figure A.

A *Represents the ship ready finished, with all things in motion.*
B *The fire wheele which moveth the rowler, and carryeth the girt whereon the figures are placed.*
C *The figures placed on the girt being in motion.*
D D D *The tier of guns which fire as the wheele beginneth to st and still.*
E E *The figures which stand ready to runne up the cords; also you may see some in their motion halfe way, and others being got up to the top of the masts.*

CHAP. LX.

How to make the Siren or Mermaid, playing on the water.

His is to be formed divers waies, according to the magnitude of the figure; if you will make one of an ordinary length, which is five or sixe foot, proceed as followeth: Let the body bee made of light rods, such as basket-makers use, and in the center of the body, let there be placed an axeltree, having too wheeles comming into the water; yet so as they may not be seene; these wheeles must be made hollow, to containe a quantity of sand or water; the use of it is to keepe the Sirene upright, and also to sinke it so farre into the water as is needfull, and likewise to make it goe more steady; note that these wheeles must bee loose, and the axeltree fast; in the midst of this axeltree, place three or foure great rockets, one by another with their mouthes all one way, yet so provide, that there may be such a diftance betweene each rocket, that there may come a vent from the taile of the firft, to the mouth of the fecond, and from the fecond to the third, and to the end that it may continue the longer in motion, you may place divers lights about the body, to make it more beautifull; every of each light extinguifhing, fhall give a report, and fo conclude. The forme of this is reprefented in the 17. Figure by the letter B.

B *Reprefents a Siren on the water.*
C *The wheeles which are loofe on the axeltree, being hollow, and filled halfe with fand or water.*
D D *The rockets placed in the axeltree which is faft.*

There are many other workes to be performed on the water, by manuall art, or the helpe of the hand : fome of which I will fhew, the reft I fhall leave to the iudgement of judicious workemen in that art; in regard there are fea fights, which are performed by gallies placed on the water, with the helpe of Mariners acted; and likewife Caftles placed both on the water, and on the fhoare; all which doe reprefent fome former ftory of the like: yet know this, there are many motions, to be wrought by hand, after a more fecret manner, which will caufe more admiration, and is done by certaine lines placed under the fuperficies of the water, the ground of which I will fhew you.

CHAP. LXI.

How to reprefent a Dragon iffuing out of a Caftle, which fhall fwimme thorow the water, and be incountred by a horfeman from the fhoare.

Aufe a Caftle to be made on certaine timber, fo as it may flote, if it be in a flowing and ebbing water, and let the bottome of the doore of this Caftle, with the ground plat, be two foot under the horizon of the water (the reafons follow) and at a foot high within the Caftle, let there bee a certaine line tyed, which may paffe thorow the body of the Dragon, and may bee faftened neere the fhoare, where you fhall have a floate likewife funke fo farre under water, that the line may not be perceived, then faften on your Dragon, as I have formerly fhewed you for the line, but fo that the head of this may alwaies be above the line, where that was under: then when the time appointed comes, there fhall be one ready within the Caftle to fire thofe parts of the Dragon which is requifite, which being done by the helpe of thofe pullies, fhall paffe it thorow the water, which fo foone as it prefents it felfe, *Neptune* (as being difpleafed to fee fo monftrous a creature within his bounds) fhall come and encounter the faid Dragon,

and

and at laft fhall overthrow him: you may order your work fo, that which you pleafe fhall have the victory, for that which keepeth fire longeft, is fuppofed to have the beft, and that which is fooneft fpent, to have the worft. Many rare things may be done in this for the pleafure of Princes, which are to be acted on the water, which for brevity fake I omit: onely I fhall fhew you the order of compofing two forts of workes, the one to be acted on the land, the other on the water. The forme of this worke is reprefented in the 17 Figure, by the letters **C D**.

G *Reprefenting the Caftle floating on the water, out of which the Dragon iffueth.*

E *The Dragon comming forth of the Caftle.*

D Neptune *comming towards the faid Dragon to encounter him.*

F *The pully which caufeth thefe motions by meanes of drawing them to and from each other: the manner of faftening the line for drawing them, I have fhewed you before in the 33 Chapter.*

CHAP. LXII.

An order for a generall piece of fire-worke for land, and is for the pleafure of a Prince or fome great perfon.

Aufe a frame to be made of wood, which let be eight fquare, or more properly eight fided (which is the beft figure for this purpofe) and let it bee forty yards from one fide to the other, there place two Caftles the one oppofite to the other, which Caftles fhall be eight foot fquare, thefe Caftles fhall be fitted with motions, as I have formerly fhewed you, fome comming out againft others, fome moving on the walles; all which may bee performed by the helpe of large fire wheeles, which muft be at the leaft fixe foot diameter, with large Rockets for the fame purpofe, as I have formerly fhewed you: then on the foure adjacent fides, you fhall place foure other wheeles, two running horizontall, and two verticall; and on the other two fides you fhall place rockets, fome flying upright, and others circular; at each angle or corner, there fhall be placed a torch of a beautifull fire and flow; fo much for the fides: now you fhall come to fill up the vacuum betweene the fides, alwaies noting that from one Caftle to the other, paffeth a frame of wood, the ufe whereof I have formerly fhewed, then before the midft of this frame, there is placed on the one fide, two fquare cafes of rockets, and betweene thefe cafes toward the bottome, and fomewhat before, there is placed anticke motions, and to the angles of each Caftle are placed two lines, with runners which take fire, and paffe to and fro; note the end of thofe lines muft be perfect wyer, or elfe the fire would burne them, then on the fame fide behinde the motions, fhall ftand aloft a frame with the Kings name or the like; then on the other fide of the frame,

within

within the vacuum, shall be placed three standing wheeles, whereof the one shall cast forth rockets into the ayre, the other two are for reports and fisgigs; these three wheeles shall stand in a triangular forme, and shall have a frame passe from the one to the other; and betweene the angles of these wheeles, shall be placed two mortar pieces, which shall bee to cast fire bats, with divers workes in them. The manner of this is represented in the 18 Figure.

CHAP. LXIII.

Another order for a generall worke, and is to be acted on the water.

Aving a place appointed for your worke, (which must be in some spacious River) you shall seeke the most convenient place on the shoare for placing a Castle, which shall bee made to represent some City or Fort lying on the water, this Castle shall be furnished with all manner of workes, as well fire bals, as rockets, with divers small Ordnance to give a more grace to the worke; this being provided, you shall also make another Castle on the water, on certain boats chained and lying at anchor, these shall bee set at a reasonable distance from the other, about twenty score, or as your place will permit: in this Castle likewise you shall provide workes, as in the other, onely this Castle may not be so big as that on shoare, then you shall provide divers small ships, which shall be ready to make a sea fight: these shall be so divided, that the greater part may belong to the smaller Castle on the water, and likewise for surprising that on the land; likewise you may have motions passing from one Castle to another, as I have formerly shewed you for the water; amongst the rest you shall have some small fire ship, such as I have shewed you, which shall have divers motions: now there are many actions to be performed by these workes, as casting bals from one Castle to the other, with the morter pieces, likewise sending backe rockets to each other, with divers onsets on each side for surprisa's, all which I leave to the discretion and appointment of the iudicious workeman; and because I will not trouble you with prolixity, I will conclude this my Pyrotechnia; onely I will at last impart that which is not the least, which is the making of certaine Engines for trying of powder, of which I shall shew you foure, with the use of them in the ensuing Chapters, and so conclude.

CHAP: LXIV.

Of the use of certain Engins for the trying of the goodnesse or strength of powder.

Efore I come to explaine the manner of making thofe Engins, I will fhew you the commodioufneffe of them, efpecially in thefe works ; for hee that will make a good rocket, muft be certain of the ftrength of his powder, which if it bee too ftrong, will break ; if too weak, it will not rife to that heighth it fhould ; which, I muft confeffe, hath been a great loffe of labour to me, as well as to other men, yet if men will be fo carefull and take that paines for the trying their powder, they may make rockets infallible ; therefore I advife every man that will work fure, firft to take his powder, be it what it will, and allay it according to the rules prefcribed, then take a quantity of that mixture, and put it into your Engin being exactly weighed to a graine, then drive your rocket, and be fure to follow the former rules prefcribed in driving your rockets, which being finifhed, with his works upon his head, you may fire ir, which if you fhall finde to bee too violent, you may allay by putting thereto a proportion of coale, and fo try it again, till fuch time you finde it to be the beft, then note that proportion for all rockets of that fize, and fo do for all others ; and if you finde your mixture yet too weak, adde thereto a fmall quantity of roch peter till you make it of fufficient ftrength ; and thus doing, you fhall have a certain and infallible rule for your proportions : I could fet down the proportions according to my Engins, but that would prove an abfurdity, in regard every Engin may have a greater or leffer ftrength added to his fprings, or the like, as you fhall perceive in the next Chapter.

CHAP. LXV.

The manner of making the aforefaid Engines for trying the ftrength of powder.

HE firft is made in a circular form, with a neck comming from the circumference, which ferves for a lid to the powder box, which box fhall bee made to hold the quantity of a dram of powder, or there about, fo that being covered with the lid, and fired, will blow, according to the ftrength of the powder, and moving, will turn about a circle of braffe, which is divided into certain equall parts, and fo will fhew the ftrength according to the part it cutteth ; for the greater the degree is that it is blown

up

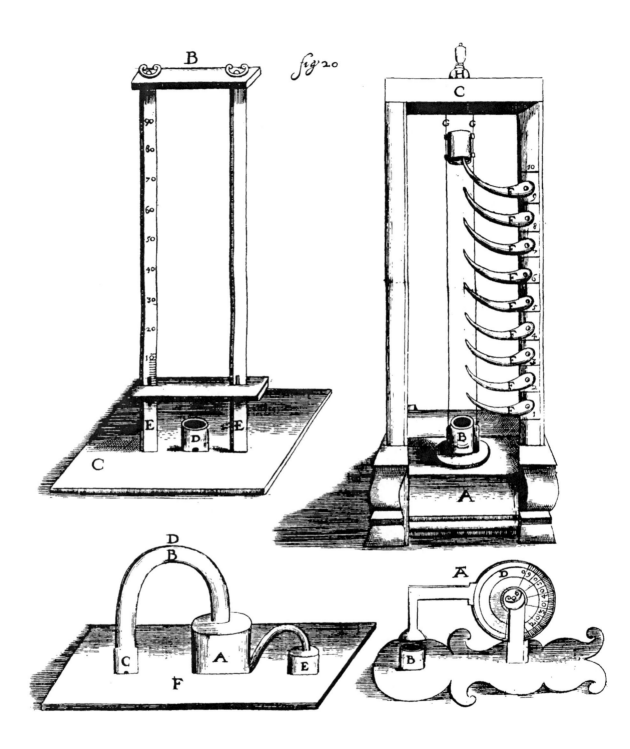

fig 20

up to, the ſtronger is the powder, and contrary. The form of this is re-preſented in the twentieth Figure, by the letter A.

A repreſenting the form of the whole Engin.
B the powder box, which muſt be filled to the top.
C the lid, which muſt be put on the ſayd box, it being filled.
D the circle of braſſe to which the lid is faſtned, which is divided into de-grees, and runneth upon the pin E, paſſing thorow the center, with a ſcrew to ſet it harder or eaſier.

CHAP. LXVI.

Another Engin for trying of powder.

HE lid of this ſecond ſort is made to riſe in a ſtraight line, and hath for his guide two ſquare pillars of braſſe, divided into degrees, with ſprings to keep it ſteaddy in this motion ; this muſt be made on a ſquare peece of braſſe, with the ſmall box in the midſt, and two ſquare pillars on each ſide, with a peece of braſſe to ſlide up and down by thoſe pillars, and muſt ſerve for a cover for your powder box ; this peece of braſſe muſt have ſmall ſprings, which muſt go to each ſide of the ſquare to guide it ſteaddy in the moti-on. The form whereof you ſhall finde in the twentieth Figure, by the letter B.

B the whole frame, with his parts adjoyned.
C the ſquare plate of braſſe, on which all is faſtned.
D the powder box, ſtanding in the midſt of that plate.
E E the two ſquare pillars of braſſe, ſtanding on this foot, and may bee made to ſcrew off and on at pleaſure.
F the lid to the fire-box, which is made to ſlide up the two ſquare pillars.
G G the ſprings, which are faſtned to the lid, to make it move more ſteaddy.
The diviſions 10, 20, &c. ſhew of what ſtrength the powder is, for the higher that the lid riſeth, the ſtronger is the powder.

CHAP. LXVII.

A third Engin for trying the ſtrength of powder.

HE third ſort are made ſomewhat after the manner of the former, which is to riſe up ſtraight, only it hath a cover hollow as big as the box, and on each ſide of the cover is a ſmall hole for a wyer to paſſe thorow, and on one of the ſides are little peeces of ſteele or braſſe, ſo fitted, that they will riſe with a touch, and give way to the riſing of the lid, and ſo ſoon as it is paſt, will hold it there, and will not ſuffer
it

it to paſſe down any further ; this I hold to bee the beſt of the three, in regard that the ſprings in the former are ſubiect to grow foule with uſe, and ſo will be very ſtiffe, every time more and more ; but this will not. The forme of this is repreſented in the twentieth Figure, by the letter C.

A *the foot whereon the Engin ſtandeth.*
B *the powder box, which hath two ſmall wyers paſſing from each ſide to the top, to guide the lid.*
D *the lid, which hath alſo two holes on each ſide for the wyers to paſſe thorow.*
E *the ſide which is divided, on which is placed at every degree, one of thoſe peeces to ſlide up and catch the lid.*
F F *the forme of thoſe catches, being either of ſteele or braſſe.*
G G *the two wyers which guide the lid of the box, and muſt bee put into a little peece of braſſe at the top, which may bee ſcrewed higher or lower, at pleaſure, for the ſtraightning of the ſame.*
H *the ſcrew which ſtraightneth thoſe wyers.*

CHAP. LXVIII.

Another Engin for trying the ſtrength of powder by water.

HE fourth, and moſt certaineſt way of all, is by water, and is thus ; cauſe a ſmall veſſell to be made of braſſe, and very tight, ſo as it may containe a pinte of water ; let this veſſell bee made in a cillindricall form, and from the top of this veſſell let there bee made a pipe of braſſe, which ſhall turne like the ſiphon, and ſhall have a ſcrew at the lower end, to ſcrew into a box of braſſe ; all which ſhall ſtand on a woodden frame : now when you wil uſe this, you ſhal fil this great veſſel halfe ſul of water, at a pipe which ſhal come from the bottom, and come up to the top winding, then ſhal there be likewiſe another veſſel underneath for a receiver, ſo that putting a quantity of powder into the ſmal box, and ſcrewing it on, it is ready ; then fire the powder, and you ſhal ſee it ſend forth a quantity of water, which you ſhall weigh, and ſo keep the weight of it, by this you ſhal know what quantity of powder of ſuch a goodneſſe wil ſend forth ſuch a quantity of water ; this I hold to be the certaineſt way, although the moſt troubleſome. The form of it is repreſented in the twentieth Figure, by the letter D.

A *repreſenting the veſſell of water, which ſhall be alwayes filled one halfe.*
B *the pipe of braſſe which paſſeth from the powder box to the veſſell of water.*
C *the powder box, being ſcrewed to one end of the ſaid pipe.*
E *the receiver, to receive ſuch water as is forced out.*
G *the pipe which conveyeth that water into the receiver.*
F *the bottom being of wood, with a plate of braſſe let into it.*

FINIS.

Printed in the United Kingdom by
Lightning Source UK Ltd., Milton Keynes
138238UK00001B/34/P